CROSSROADS
READINGS IN SOCIAL PROBLEMS

A Customized Sociology Reader

General Editor
Kathleen A. Tiemann
University of North Dakota

Compiled by

Pamela Hunt
Social Problems
SOC 22778
Kent State University

PEARSON
Custom
Publishing

Director of Database Publishing: Michael Payne
Sponsoring Editor: Robin J. Lazrus
Development Editor: Catherine O'Keefe
Editorial Assistant: Ana Díaz-Caneja
Marketing Manager: Kathleen Kourian
Operations Manager: Eric M. Kenney
Production Project Manager: Marianne C. Groth
Database Project Specialist: Elizabeth MacKenzie-Lamb
Rights Editor: Francesca Marcantonio
Cover Designer: Seamus Culligan and Renée Sartell

Cover Art: "Crowded City Street with Arrow Symbol," courtesy of Tony Stone Images/Chicago, Inc.
"Simultaneous Formation," courtesy of Robin MacDonald-Foley.

Printed in the United States of America

Please visit our website at *www.pearsoncustom.com*
Attention bookstores: For permission to return any unsold stock, contact Pearson Custom Publishing at 1-800-777-6872.

ISBN: 0536142289

PEARSON CUSTOM PUBLISHING
75 Arlington St., Suite 300
Boston, MA 02116

Preface

> *. . . There are, of course, different ways of looking at social problems, and...these perspectives reflect the tension that has existed since sociology first developed—the tension between concentrating on the problems of society, on the one hand, and on the development of sociology as a scientific discipline, on the other . . .*
>
> Earl Rubington and Martin S. Weinberg

Pearson Custom Publishing and General Editor Kathleen A. Tiemann are proud to bring you *Crossroads; Readings in Social Problems.*

Our highest goal in the creation of *Crossroads* is to give you the opportunity to show your students that there are 'different ways of looking at social problems.' A traditional way of doing this has been to expose students to central sociological ideas and examples of sociology in action through a book of readings. While *Crossroads* is a reader, it is anything but traditional due to the way it is being provided to you.

With *Crossroads*, we have endeavored to provide you with a rich and diverse archive of high quality readings in such a way that both professors and students will have easy and cost-effective access to the minds and ideas that illuminate and help explain some of the central ideas and issues in the study of social problems. Within *Crossroads* you will find over 270 readings—which we will update and expand yearly—from which you can choose only those readings that are germane to your particular course. No longer will you and your students have to be dependent on the standard large and expensive 'one-size-fits-all' college reader, which often includes more material than will be covered in the course, yet often also lacks those particular pieces that are viewed as essential by individual instructors. In addition, a classification system for each selection provides helpful information on how the selections might be organized to allow the various perspectives on the course to be pursued. Although the primary course for which *Crossroads* was developed is the introductory social problems course, the size and quality of the database may also make it a good resource for a variety of other courses such as introduction to sociology, marriage and family, and gender studies.

However it is used, it is our ultimate hope that you will find *Crossroads* to be an essential source of readings in social problems—a source noted for its depth, breadth, and flexibility—that meets the highest scholarly and pedagogical standards.

Acknowledgements

A project of this scope cannot be undertaken without the assistance and advice of our colleagues. The project idea and execution was reviewed several times as it was being developed, and each of the following provided valuable feedback and suggestions, which strengthened the project greatly.

A project of this scope cannot be undertaken without the assistance and advice of our colleagues. The project idea and execution was reviewed several times as it was being developed, and each of the following provided valuable feedback and suggestions, which strengthened the project greatly.

Judy Aulette, *University of North Carolina, Charlotte*; Lorenzo M. Boyd, *Old Dominion University*; Cynthia J. Crivaro, *Northern Essex Community College*; Frank Elwell, *Rogers State University*; Marcia J. Ghidina, *University of North Carolina at Asheville*; Idolina Hernandez, *Cy-Fair College*; Thomas Hood, *University of Tennessee*; Shirley A. Jackson, *Southern Connecticut State University*; Dave Khey, *University of Florida*; Rhonda Dean Kyncl, *University of Oklahoma*; Gregory C. Leavitt, *Idaho State University*; Russell Long, *Del Mar College*; Philip Luck, *Georgia State University*; Dana Mayhew, *Bristol Community College*; Kimberly McGann, *Finger Lakes Community College/SUNY Geneseo*; Phoebe Morgan, *Northern Arizona University*; Joan T. Olson, *University of Mary Washington*; Barbara Perry, *Northern Arizona University*; Anne Peterson, *Columbus State Community College*; Karl Pfeiffer, *University of Alaska, Anchorage*; Frank A. Salamone, *Iona College*; Stuart Shafer, *Johnson County Community College*; Ira Silver, *Framingham State College*; Dave Smith, *University of California, Irvine*; Ronald L. Stubbs, *Florida International University*; Linda Toonen, *University of Wisconsin at Green Bay*; Bradley Wing, *University of Missouri Columbia*; R. Dean Wright, *Drake University*; Michelle Worosz, *Michigan State University*; Mary Lou Wylie, *James Madison University*.

We welcome your feedback at any time on *Crossroads*. Please simply send comments and suggestions to www.dbasepub@pearsoncustom.com.

e
o
di
co
ger

Contents

v

The Sociological Imagination and Social Problems

KATHLEEN A. TIEMANN

© © © ©

"Global Trafficking in Women Increases"

"Homeless on $50,000 a Year"

"Child Abducted"

"Over Half of All Americans Are Obese"

"Child Shoots Classmate for Teasing"

"Defective Firestone Tires Linked to Accidents in Ford Explorer"

*E*very day, we are bombarded with headlines like these, whether in the newspapers or on TV news reports. We might agree that selling women, being homeless, abducting children, being obese, shooting someone in retaliation for teasing, and putting unsafe products on the market are morally wrong, unhealthy, or socially undesirable. But does each really constitute a social problem? When does an individual or a group's concerns collectively become a social problem?

The work of American sociologist C. Wright Mills can help us address this question. Mills believed that sociology's main purpose should be to understand the relationship between individuals and the society in which they live. To begin grasping the nature of this relationship, Mills believed, we need to develop a quality of mind that he called the sociological imagination. Simply stated, our sociological imagination lets us see the effect of social forces such as economic struggle or attitudes toward gender on our private lives. By using our sociological imagination, we can understand how social, historical, cultural, economic, and political factors shape the choices that people make and the ways in which they live their lives. This helps us shift our attention from blaming victims of social problems for their suffering. Instead, we can identify the structural causes of suffering—that is, the elements of our social system that create problems. And by recognizing the structural sources of social problems, we can join with others to change the aspects of our society that spawn these difficulties.

The sociological imagination helps us distinguish between what Mills called "private troubles" and "public issues." Private troubles, he explained, affect individuals and their immediate relations with others. Therefore, if homelessness, child abduction, or obesity creates a problem for an individual or for scattered individuals, it is a private trouble. While private troubles are painful for those who experience them, they are not necessarily social problems.

In contrast to personal troubles, public issues go beyond the individual and threaten some widely held value within a society. Accordingly, if homelessness, child abduction, or obesity becomes widespread because of underemployment, poverty, a high divorce rate, or other social forces—and it affects large numbers of people in a region, state, or society—it becomes a public issue, or social problem. By applying our sociological imagination, we can recognize how the events we experience as personal troubles often originate from specific historical and social conditions. Stated differently, developing a sociological imagination helps us grasp the complex sources of our difficulties and make sense of our lives. For example, homeless people in the United States aren't necessarily homeless because they're lazy; they may be homeless in large part because numerous corporations have moved their facilities to other countries where labor costs are lower, and because of this, have laid off countless U.S. workers.

☙ The History of Sociology and the Study of Social Problems

The discipline of sociology grew out of concern over the social problems that cropped up in England and Europe primarily as a result of the Industrial Revolution. Among other things, the rise of industry spurred urbanization, immigration, and overcrowding in cities. The traditional social order began to collapse as the new middle class began to insist on democracy. This collapse in turn catalyzed the French and American revolutions—both of which toppled century-old aristocracies and monarchies. The two revolutions stressed the notion of equality, a belief that rational thought could ease the horrendous social conditions that had arisen, and a new image of humanitarianism and human nature (Rose, 1971).

August Comte (1798-1857), the man who gave sociology its name, and his followers strongly influenced this development. In Comte's time, social critics focused on the scientific aspects of social problems and the emergence of what was known as a positivistic social order. To positivists, social facts matter the most in our analysis of social problems. Thus, researchers sought to produce an "objective" analysis of social phenomena by using research methods and models based on the natural sciences.

Other Europeans who influenced the early development of sociology include:

Karl Marx, who strove to alleviate problems that he attributed to capitalism;

Emile Durkheim, whose work centered on establishing and maintaining social order;

3

Max Weber, who tried to create a foundation for "meaningful sociology" by writing extensively on the philosophy and methods of the social sciences and the role of the researcher's values (Rose, 1971); and

Harriet Martineau, who paved the way for the study of sociology in the United States by translating Comte's works into English, conducted pioneering sociological studies, and wrote the first known research-methods book in sociology (Hill, 1991).

Sociology crossed the Atlantic Ocean in the late 1800s; the first college course in the field was offered at Yale University in 1876. The University of Chicago, which established the first department of sociology in 1893, became a major hub of sociological activity in the United States. In this country, the impetus for studying social problems initially came from reform-minded, moralistic, and anti-urban individuals (Rose, 1971). Early American sociologists were thus often ministers, the sons of ministers, social workers, or members of reform groups who viewed sociology as a tool for resolving the most dire problems of the day (Hartjen, 1977). These sociologists took what's called a social-pathology approach to such problems. Because this view assumed that ethical deficiencies in people caused social problems, it focused on catalyzing individual rather than institutional change.

As you might well imagine, C. Wright Mills criticized this perspective, pointing out that social pathology was a professional ideology that grew out of the religious, rural, middle-class backgrounds of its proponents. Mills also maintained that pathologists dealt with fragmented problems rather than seeing their interconnections and their links to the social structure. Moreover, social pathologists saw social problems as violations of a society's moral expectations and thus the results of inadequate socialization. While they initially believed that this failure was inherent in people, they later attributed it to the social environment. Thus, Mills lamented, the social-pathology approach encouraged people to address humanitarian concerns without tackling the true root of social problems: social structure.

Between 1920 and 1940, sociologists paid less attention to social problems. This was in part a reaction against the reformist orientation of many who studied social problems. However, it also stemmed from the low status given to sociology by other academics and the general public (Rose, 1971). To protect their fragile credibility, sociologists avoided any applications-based research that might further diminish the scientific standing of the discipline, and instead focused on theory work (Hartjen, 1977).

The field experienced a major trauma during this period: a split between the theoretical or "pure" sociology done primarily by men at the University of Chicago and the applied sociology being done for the most part by women at Hull House, the second major hub of sociological activity in Chicago. Because many female sociologists took the unpopular position of pacifism before, during, and even after World War II, the women of Hull House drew criticism for their "radical" ideas on peace and war from many sectors, including other sociologists, the general public, and the government. In 1918, "a massive, male-orchestrated erosion of [the Hull House women's] thought and practice [had] ensued and . . . female sociologists were pushed out of sociology" (Deegan, 1988, p. 144). The discipline ignored their contributions. As a result, the women of Hull House began moving into other fields, including social work.

During World War II, sociologists took a newly active, but involuntary, role in addressing social problems when the federal government called on them to collect and analyze data on war-related problems like civilian and military morale, turnover in the workplace, and postwar adjustments of soldiers and civilians (Hartjen, 1977; Curran & Renzetti, 1996). This task helped shift sociologists' role from that of social reformers to "value-free" scientists. As a result, the discipline garnered new credibility and respect as a science. Moreover, sociology's new reputation somewhat eased the long-time feud between the applied and pure-science movements that had manifested itself in the tension between the men of the Chicago

School and the women of Hull House (Rose, 1971). In 1950, sociologists would establish the Society for the Study of Social Problems, which further burnished their professional image (Rose, 1971).

After World War II, sociologists turned even further away from the social-pathology position and moved toward a more scientific orientation that emphasized methodology. All of this aimed to further shore up their standing as scientists. The sociology department at the University of Chicago and the social-disorganization perspective it advocated played an instrumental part in this shift (Rose, 1971). These sociologists borrowed from biology to develop a model of urban life. They used this model to study the growth of cities, the lifestyles of the people who lived there, and the effects of social change on everyday life. Advocates of this perspective regarded society as a system whose parts worked together. When social change occurs and the traditional values, norms, and rules that govern daily life no longer appear to apply, social disorganization results. According to this perspective, the solution to social problems is to bring the system back into a state of equilibrium.

During the early 1950s, as in earlier eras, books on social problems reflected the preoccupations of the times. Thus, sociologists riveted their attention on issues such as McCarthyism and the communist threat. In offering solutions to social problems, sociologists suggested gradual and realistic reform guided by experts. The field thus became more professionalized in this era and began to blend theory, research, and application. Sociology had become a respected science (Rubington & Weinberg, 1995).

Nevertheless, by the mid-1950s, sociologists began to recognize that their emphasis on theoretical questions had made them neglect the very social issues they wanted to resolve. They realized that like their social-pathology predecessors, they had become agents of the status quo (Rubington & Weinberg, 1995). Thus, sociologists began to redirect their attention to social issues of the day.

In the 1960s, the study of social problems in the United States centered on the impact of individuals' being marginalized by the cultural mainstream. Researchers believed that social problems would ease if the technological and intellectual resources of established U.S. institutions could be extended to underdeveloped regions like Appalachia and disadvantaged groups like African-Americans. This inclusion, they maintained, could be achieved through large-scale governmental programs (Skolnick & Currie, 1997). One program that grew out of this effort was the 1964 War on Poverty instituted by U.S. president Lyndon B. Johnson.

The tensions within the field that had originated in the late 1950s escalated during the 1960s and peaked in the 1970s. During that decade, sociologist Alvin Gouldner argued that sociology no longer had any value in a society that was increasingly mired in crisis. Gouldner urged a more critical point of view to vanquish the problems plaguing both U.S. society and the field of sociology. Specifically, he suggested a Marxist approach to social problems. This approach had at its center a critique of capitalism, by which the "haves" protect what they possess at the expense of the "have-nots." Gouldner's views helped restore a broader perspective and reconnected the field with its European roots. Moreover, this shift in perspective helped move the discipline forward by shaking it out of its complacency (Rubington & Weinberg, 1995).

Still, attitudes toward social problems in the 1970s and 1980s proved much harsher than they had been previously. In the 1960s, U.S. citizens and policy makers had believed that most social problems were solvable, and the government had launched myriad programs and social experiments. However, when the problems refused to evaporate—despite all the money being invested in their resolution—citizens began to complain that their government had taken on too big a role. This criticism led to scholarly pessimism about social problems, and once again arguments about "inferior" people and cultures surfaced. These beliefs in turn facilitated harsher social policies, which curtailed or scaled back numerous social-welfare programs. Thus, by the 1980s, U.S. citizens' views of social problems had once again come full circle, and sociologists' work focused on "defectives, dependents, and delinquents"—just as it had in the late 1800s and early 1900s (Skolnick & Currie, 1997).

Many people believe that, despite rhetoric to the contrary, the harshness of the 1980s is still with us today. It may have softened slightly with sound bites from politicians claiming to be "compassionate conservatives" and with government pressure on local regions to take responsibility for social problems. Nevertheless, poverty, racism, pollution, and other difficulties are still with us. Moreover, no one can predict the impact that current technological innovations and economic conditions might have on social problems in the future. Clearly, many questions persist, and the field of sociology continues to experience ups and downs as it evolves.

☙ Understanding Social Problems

While C. Wright Mills provided some answers to the questions of what constitutes a social problem and how such problems should be tackled, contemporary sociologists have a variety of other ideas. For example, a traditional perspective treats social problems as objective conditions that exist within a society. To illustrate, one contemporary social-problems textbook defines a social problem as "a social condition (such as poverty) or a pattern of behavior (such as substance abuse) that people believe warrants public concern and collective action to bring about change" (Kendall, 1998, p. 2). Another text defines a social problem as "a condition caused by factors endemic to a particular society that disadvantages or harms a specific segment or a significant number of the society's population" (Curran & Renzetti, 1996, p. 3). Both definitions present social problems as undesirable conditions or behaviors of some magnitude that people can readily count, touch, or observe.

Those who subscribe to the objective-conditions perspective ask three main questions:

* What is the nature, extent, and distribution of the problem?

- What causes the problem?
- How can the problem be controlled or prevented?

The objective-conditions perspective is satisfying to many nonsociologists because it fits their commonsense understanding of what constitutes a social problem: It is real, it is undesirable, it harms many people, and the problem must be solved for the greater good.

Let's use the issue of poverty in the United States to illustrate how an objectivist might make sense of a social problem. Objectivists would first want to know the nature and extent of poverty. Therefore, they could count the number of people who fall below the poverty line. As such, they might discover that some 13 percent, or roughly 38 million U.S. citizens, are officially poor (U.S. Bureau of the Census, 1997). Objectivists could also describe the circumstances of the poor in concrete terms. For example, they could define poor people as those who:

- live in substandard housing or homeless shelters,
- lack adequate clothing and food,
- lack access to medical care, and
- have little opportunity for a high-quality life.

In addition to these criteria, objectivists would note that many poor people are elderly, or are children who live in single-parent households. Moreover, the poor disproportionately comprise people of color and people who reside in the southern United States and rural areas.

And what causes poverty? Objectivists might answer: unemployment, underemployment, inadequate education, divorce, substance abuse, mental and physical illness, and discrimination.

Finally, how can this problem be controlled or eliminated? Some answers seem obvious, and most, if not all, require money. For example, representatives of local, state, and federal government can work to bring good paying jobs to those who need them, offer greater access to education, establish affordable child care for single parents, set up programs to help those with addictions or mental disorders, and educate people about the social costs of discrimination.

Other sociologists embrace a social-constructionist perspective. They see social problems not as objective conditions, but as concerns defined as such by people. Therefore, instead of emphasizing conditions or behaviors, social constructionists focus on the process by which people designate some real or imagined social conditions, but not others, as social problems. As one sociology author wrote, "Our sense of what is or is not a social problem is a product, something that has been produced or constructed through social activities" (Best, 1995, p. 6).

The most influential statement on the social-constructionist perspective appears in a classic book titled *Constructing Social Problems*, by Malcolm Spector and John I. Kitsuse. In this book, the authors define social problems as "the activities of individuals or groups making assertions of grievances and claims with respect to some putative [imagined] conditions" (Spector & Kitsuse, 1977/1987, p. 75). Whether harmful, annoying, or dangerous conditions or behavior actually exist is irrelevant; according to this perspective, a social problem does not exist until someone defines it and responds to it as such.

Physical violence toward children provides an apt illustration of this perspective. At various times and in several geographical areas, the use of physical violence toward children has been commonplace. Parents and teachers have used it to secure young people's obedience toward their mothers and fathers or toward God, and as a means of discipline. Moreover, the Roman legal code of "Patria Patistas" and English common law made this practice legal in earlier eras in Europe (Pfohl, 1977). While the expression "child abuse" was first documented in medical literature in 1888 (Solomon, 1973), it was not designated as a social problem in the United States until the 1960s, owing to a now-famous article on the "battered-child syndrome" published in the *Journal of the American Medical Association* (Kempe, Silverman, Stelle, Droegemuller, & Silver, 1962). This article described the characteristic injuries suffered by children under the age of three at the hands of their parents. The publication of this article, and the accompanying editorial that asserted the seriousness of the problem, legitimized child abuse as a social problem. Because the syndrome was now defined as a social problem, states began passing laws designed to stop child abuse. Many of these laws were put in place during the period 1962-1966 (Pfohl, 1977). Thus "child abuse," though it had existed for centuries without being defined as a social problem, now had a place on the public's social-problem "radar screen."

❧ Solving Social Problems

Can social problems be solved? Yes, but the attempt to solve them constitutes a problem in itself. Four difficulties hamper this effort:

1. Major social problems are deeply rooted in our culture and the social structure. Therefore, by the time we define or recognize something as a social problem, it has already been institutionalized. For example, many people ignored warnings about an impending energy crisis until 1979, when summer gasoline shortages spawned interminable lines at gas stations. The shortages caused U.S. citizens to temporarily change their ways. Families took vacations closer to home, and politicians looked for ways to release the country from its dependence on oil-producing nations. For example, the federal government instituted fuel-efficiency standards that required auto manufacturers to create more fuel-efficient vehicles.

However, in the 1980s, the abundance of relatively inexpensive fuel that resulted from these changes once again made people complacent. Under the Reagan and Bush presidential administrations, the country abandoned many of these policies. Not surprisingly, auto manufacturers began building less fuel-efficient cars. Sales of trucks and sports utility vehicles (SUVs) soared. By 2000, U.S. motorists once again felt the pinch at the gas station when fuel costs rose owing to a greater demand for gasoline than suppliers could provide. Will we again turn to policies that encourage energy independence and fuel-efficient vehicles, or will we instead ravage fragile environmental areas to gain access to untapped oil reserves? In either case, we would still be ignoring the institutionalized roots of the problem.

2. All solutions to social problems have their own costs. For example, to curb air pollution caused by internal-combustion engines, the government could heavily tax people for their use of private automobiles. This would encourage the use of more environmentally sound means of getting around, such as public transportation, walking, or bicycle riding. However, this solution exacts personal, political, economic, and social costs. Heavily taxing cars would put a burden on people living on fixed incomes, individuals who need their vehicles to make a living, those with physical disabilities, and others who can't easily get to bus, subway, or railway stations. Moreover, many communities' public-transportation systems wouldn't be able to accommodate the flood of new passengers that such taxation would create. Additionally, those who make their living by providing services related to the auto industry would likely lose their jobs. Thus, addressing the problems created by this one solution to air pollution would require considerable money.

3. Solutions to social problems are controversial. One reason that a solution may generate controversy is that it may translate into gains for some groups but costs for others. If we continue with the example above, we can see that heavily taxing private automobiles would likely result in fewer car sales. That would prompt the closure of auto plants and service facilities and put many people out of work. However, industries involved in the production of buses, high-speed rail transport, and bicycles would get a boost, as would those that provide the infrastructure for the use of these means of transportation. For example, existing track would need repair to handle the new demands, new track would have to be laid, more workers would be required, etc.

4. Social problems are interrelated and complex. For instance, if the U.S. government cuts taxes to give people more disposable income, the money available for social-welfare programs shrinks. If the government spends money developing public transportation because owning private automobiles is too costly for most citizens, auto workers lose their jobs. These workers thus become eligible for unemployment benefits, which in turn require more tax dollars. Similarly, if a company that is struggling to compete in the global economy opens a plant in another country where labor is cheaper and environmental restrictions are less rigorous, U.S. workers may lose their jobs. Moreover, though people living in this other country are now employed, they may work under inhumane conditions. The environment of the host country may suffer irreparable damage as well.

At this point, you may well feel overwhelmed or disheartened by the difficulties posed in solving social problems. However, individuals can still play a powerful role in addressing such issues. For example, we can become active in politics and social movements and demand that our government representatives take action on issues that concern us. We can volunteer our time or give our financial support to groups like:

Habitat for Humanity, which seeks to eliminate substandard housing and helps low-income people become homeowners (www.hfh.org);

Greenpeace, which strives to protect the environment and avert nuclear conflict (www.greenpeace.org);

Oxfam, which funds self-help projects, provides disaster relief in poor countries, and distributes educational information on development and hunger (www.oxfam.org); and

Amnesty International, which advocates for the release of political prisoners, tries to ensure fair and prompt trials for such individuals, and seeks to curtail the torture and execution of prisoners (www.amnesty.org).

You don't have to contribute to just large-scale causes, either; you can also make a big difference by helping a few people close to home—through teaching literacy skills, volunteering at a soup kitchen or battered-women's shelter, or participating in a Big Brother/Big Sister program near you. There's plenty of work to be done, and perhaps the best way to choose from among the many opportunities to help out is to pick one or two causes that have the most meaning for you. Don't feel that you have to help everyone; you can't. But, you can make a major difference in the larger effort to address our society's biggest problems.

It may also be tempting to look to technology to solve social problems like hunger, pollution, or sexually transmitted diseases. Technology certainly has its place and has allowed us to solve some social problems in the past. For example, science eradicated childhood polio, and new devices in the home (such as microwave ovens) make life easier for busy people. But as politicians, scientists, and ordinary citizens alike have begun to realize, technology has also directly caused some of the social problems we face today. For example, our dependence on the internal-combustion engine has created dense pockets of air pollution across the globe. And our increased reliance on electrically powered devices in our daily lives has ratcheted up our demand for electricity. As a result, we're running out of affordable, environmentally friendly sources of electricity—as happened in California in the early months of 2001. Clearly, while technology can solve some social problems, it also spawns new ones.

☙ ☙ ☙

The articles in this anthology describe a wide range of social problems—and an equally wide range of views on them. As you read these selections, try to determine which of the above perspectives the various authors subscribe to. And, think about how the use of these perspectives might affect the authors' presentation of issues. Finally, think about how the authors' and your own views on social problems influence your responses to the issues addressed in the articles.

References

Best, J. (1995). *Images of issues.* Hawthorne, NY: Aldine de Gruyter.

Curran, D.J., & Renzetti, C.M. (1996). *Social problems: Society in crisis.* Boston: Allyn and Bacon.

Hartjen, C.A. (1977). *Possible trouble: An analysis of social problems.* New York: Praeger.

Hill, M.R. (1991). Harriet Martineau (1802-1876). In M.J. Deegan (Ed), *Women in sociology: A bio-bibliographical sourcebook* (pp. 289-297). New York: Greenwood.

Kempe, C.H., Silverman, F.N., Stelle, B.F., Droegemuller, W., & Silver, H.K. (1962). The battered-child syndrome. *Journal of the American Medical Association, 181,* 17-24.

Kendall, D. (1998). *Social problems in a diverse society.* Boston: Allyn and Bacon.

Mills, C.W. (1959). *The sociological imagination.* New York: Oxford.

Mills, C.W. (1943). The professional ideology of social pathologists. *American Journal of Sociology, 49,* 165-180.

Pfohl, S.J. (1977). The "discovery" of child abuse. *Social Problems, 24,* 310-323.

Rose, A. (1971). History and sociology of the study of social problems. In E.O. Smigel (Ed.), *Handbook for the study of social problems.* Chicago: Rand McNally.

Skolnick, J.H., & Currie, E. (1997). *Crisis in American institutions.* New York: Longman.

Smith, J. (1981). *Social issues & the social order: The contradictions of capitalism.* Cambridge, MA: Winthrop Publishing.

Solomon, T. (1973). History and demography of child abuse. *Pediatrics, 51,* 773-776.

Spector, M., & Kitsuse, J.I. (1977/1987). *Constructing social problems.* Hawthorne, NY: Aldine de Gruyter.

U.S. Bureau of the Census. (1997). Income up, health coverage down, and poverty unchanged. *Census and you*. November.

The Problem with Social Problems

DONILEEN R. LOSEKE
University of South Florida

> *Most people take a common-sense approach to social prob-
> lems. That is, they believe social problems exist as observable
> objective conditions. However, sociologist Donileen R. Loseke
> argues that viewing social problems solely as objective condi-
> tions, and ignoring subjective definitions, severely limits our
> understanding of social problems. In this excerpt from her
> book,* Thinking About Social Problems, *she introduces anoth-
> er perspective from which to view social problems—the social
> construction (or constructionist) perspective. She argues that
> by focusing on subjective definitions, we cannot only under-
> stand how people create social problems, but also how we sus-
> tain and change the meaning attributed to them.*

. . .

*I*n this last decade of the twentieth century, the American landscape is littered with social problems. That is our topic here. I'll
begin simply with a question for you, a reader of these lines: What do
you think are the ten most important social problems in the United
States today?

What is on your list? Perhaps poverty, AIDS, abortion, crime.
Your list might include problems of "abuse" (child abuse, wife abuse,
alcohol abuse, drug abuse). It could include problems of "rights"
(homosexual rights, ability-impaired peoples' rights, laboratory ani-

mal rights); it could include "isms" (racism, sexism, ageism, anti-Semitism), or problems from solutions to other problems (welfare, affirmative action, busing of school children). Your list might include institutional problems, such as problems of the economy (factory shutdowns, a lack of well-paying jobs, unemployed Black teenagers), politics (illegal campaign contributions, politicians accused of sexual harassment), family (divorce, men who don't pay child support, single mothers, teenage pregnancy), education (schools that don't teach), or medicine (lack of affordable medical care, medical malpractice). Your list might include problems of individual behavior (smoking, drinking, drugs, Satanic cults, teens who gun down classmates); it might include problems of the environment (acid rain, deforestation, loss of the ozone layer).

There are three important lessons in this small exercise of naming social problems. First, there seemingly is no end to conditions in the United States that might be called social problems. Granted, the problems of crime and poverty tend to remain on the public's and policymakers' lists of problems, and racial inequality often is called this country's most enduring social problem. But after these, the list is all but endless. If given time, you could think of more than ten problems confronting the United States today. If you compared your own list to lists made by others, the number of items would grow. What we call social problems range from conditions isolated within one or another community (a specific manufacturing plant closing down, polluted water in a particular community, UFO sightings in another), to those affecting particular regions of the country (homelessness in the Midwest because of floods, the many problems of migrant workers in California, Texas, and Florida), to problems found throughout the entire nation (AIDS, inequalities, lack of low-cost day care for children), to those that cross international borders (human rights, world hunger, overpopulation, Pakistan and India testing nuclear bombs). The list is all but endless; the list is ever changing.

A second lesson in this simple exercise of naming social problems is that social problems are about disagreements. You might believe that some of the problems I offered are not social problems at all; you might believe that I failed to mention others that are far more important. Or, you and I might be thinking about very different things even if we did agree to include something on a list of important problems. If there is a problem called "homosexual rights," for example, is this a problem of too many rights or too few? If there is a problem of "school prayer," is this a problem of too much prayer or too little? Or, we might disagree on what, particularly, should be included in the problem. Is it "date rape" if a woman says yes but means no? If a married couple who can't afford their own home must live with the wife's parents, is that an example of "homelessness?" Or, we might agree that something is a problem of a particular type and we might agree on what is included in the problem, but still we might not agree about what should be done to resolve it. So, even if we agreed that "teenage pregnancy" is a social problem, do you think we should promote sexual abstinence or provide birth control? Should we try to make life easier for teen parents so that they can remain in school, or should we make life more difficult for them in order to show others that there are negative costs to teen pregnancy? As another example, even if we agree that there is a problem of teens who take guns to school and open fire on their classmates and teachers, what causes this problem? Is it a problem of schools, of parents, of mentally unbalanced teens? Is it a problem of guns? What we should do depends on what we think causes the problem. Social problems are about disagreements.

A third lesson from this simple exercise of naming social problems is that social problems are about conditions *and* they are about people in those conditions. A social problem called crime contains two types of people: criminals and victims of crime. A social problem called poverty contains poor people. Likewise we can talk about pollution and polluters, welfare and welfare recipients, a lack of civility and uncivil people. Whether explicit and obvious (the condition of unemployment and the people who are unemployed) or implicit and subtle (the deindustrialization of America, which implies unemployed or underemployed workers), social problems include both conditions (something) and people (somebody).

Let me ask another question: Think of your list of the top ten U.S. social problems. What do all of these conditions have in common? What is a social problem? My guess is that when I asked you to name ten social problems you didn't think to yourself, "What does she mean?" In daily life, social problems are something like "pornography" in that few people can define the meaning of the term itself but most folks say they know it when they see it. So it goes with social problems. We rarely (if ever) in daily life think about what the term itself means but we have little trouble knowing a social problem when we see one. Our first task, then, is to define "social problem."

❧ What Is a Social Problem?

While writers of social problems textbooks can offer complex definitions of their topic matter, I want to focus on *public perceptions* where there seem to be general agreements. There are four parts to this most basic definition of social problems.

First, we use the term "social problem" to indicate that something is *wrong*. This is common sense. The name is social *problem* so the topic matter includes those conditions that are negative. In popular understanding, a social problem is *not* something like happy families, good health, or schools that succeed in educating children. "Social problem" is a term we use to note *trouble*.

The second part of the definition of social problems sounds harsh and uncaring: To be given the status of a social problem the condition must be *widespread,* which means that more than a few people must be hurt. If I lose my job, that is a *personal trouble*.[1] It's sad for me but not, necessarily, for you or for anyone else. But if something causes many of us to lose our jobs, then it is a social problem that wasn't created by (and therefore can't be resolved by) individuals. I like to talk about Jeffrey Dahmer to illustrate this. Jeffrey Dahmer was a man who killed—and ate—young boys. He showed Americans that there could be cannibals among us. I don't know about you, but I think that's certainly wrong. But Americans never mention the problem of cannibalism when we talk to people doing public opinion polls; cannibalism isn't mentioned in social problems texts; it's not debated in the halls of Congress; there aren't any social services to reform cannibals; we aren't asked to donate money for the cause of stopping cannibalism, and so forth. Why not? Because as hideous as it was that Jeffrey Dahmer killed and ate young boys, one cannibal among us is not enough to make cannibalism a social problem. Social problems are those troublesome conditions affecting a *significant number of people.*

Third, the definition of social problem includes a dose of optimism. Conditions called social problems share the characteristic that we think it's possible they can be *changed.* They are conditions we think are caused by humans and therefore can be changed by humans. Consider the condition of death. This certainly is a troublesome and widespread condition. But humans will die and that can't be changed. So, death isn't a social problem. At the same time, think about the many other conditions surrounding death that *could* be changed: We could possibly change *when* people die (using medical technology to extend life or assisted suicide to end life) and *how* people die (care in nursing homes for elderly people, automobile or airplane crashes that cause early death). Likewise, earthquakes or tornadoes aren't social problems because nothing can be done to stop them. But we could talk about social problems surrounding natural disasters—there are potential social problems such as the cost of insurance, failures of early-warning systems for disasters, or the response of officials to such disasters. "Social problems" is a term we use when we believe the troublesome condition *can be fixed by humans.*

A social problem is a condition defined as wrong, widespread, and changeable. The fourth and final component of the definition is that " social problem" is a name for conditions we believe *should* be changed. This is very logical. If the condition is troublesome and if it occurs frequently and if it can be changed, then it follows it should be changed. Americans tend to use the name "social problems" for conditions we believe are so troublesome that they can't be ignored. To say that something is a social problem is to take a stand that *something needs to be done.*

We use the term "social problem" to categorize troublesome conditions that are prevalent, that can be changed, that should be changed. . . . With this basic definition in hand we can go on to the next question: What should we study about social problems? This question doesn't have a simple answer because social problems are about two quite different aspects of social life: They are about *objective* conditions and people (things and people that exist in the physical world) and they are about *subjective definitions* (how we understand our world and the people in it). Because it isn't immediately and obviously apparent why the objective and subjective aspects of social problems can be separated, I'll discuss each of them.

I begin with the commonsense framework of a type of person I'll call a *practical actor*. I'll use this term when I want to refer to a type of person like you or me in our daily lives. As practical actors, we aren't academics studying something, we're simply citizens living in this country. We have jobs and/or we go to school; we're concerned with getting through our days the best ways possible. We might not have the education of a nuclear scientist, but we're not stupid; we think, we use common sense. Practical actors most often are concerned with social problems as objective conditions.

◉ Social Problems as Objective Conditions and People in the Social World

When members of the American public use the term "social problems" we are most frequently interested in these as *objective* characteristics of the social environment. "Objective" means real, tangible, measurable. Within this perspective, social problems are about things we can see; they are about measurable and widespread conditions in the environment and they are about the living, breathing people who are hurt by these conditions or who create these conditions. Within this perspective, poverty is a condition where people don't have enough money to live a decent life, and poor people are people living in this condition. Or, drunk driving is a condition where people with a high blood alcohol count drive cars, and drunk drivers are the people who do this. When we think about social problems as objective characteristics of the social environment, a series of very practical questions emerge: Who or what causes the condition? What harm is created? What types of people are harmed? What can we do to stop this harm?

When experts study social problems in this way, they rely on *objective indicators* of social problems conditions, causes, and consequences. These indicators include statistics such as those showing the numbers of school children who can't read, the numbers of crimes committed, or the number of babies born addicted to crack. There also are objective indicators of types of people who cause social problems or who are harmed by social problems. These are measures such as age, ethnicity, or gender. There also can be more complex psychological profiles: people who commit crimes are given various psychological tests and a profile of "criminals" is constructed; tests are given to heterosexuals to measure their "homophobia"; women victims of "wife abuse" are given tests and psychological profiles of "battered women" are constructed from them, and so on.

Such objective indicators are the basis of arguments in many social problems textbooks. Such texts most often are arranged in a series of chapters with titles such as "Problems in the Economy," "Problems in Government," "Problems of Inequality" (poverty, ethnicity, age, gender), "Problems of Deviance" (sexual behavior, drug use, crime), and so on. Each chapter in these texts tends to contain a more or less standardized treatment of the problem at hand. Readers see objective indicators describing the extent of the problem (how widespread it is), what people are involved in it, and the consequences of the problem for the people. Various sociological theories are used to explain the causes of the problem and this leads to statements about what can be done to resolve it.

This makes sense because practical actors are concerned with social problems as objective conditions. But now I'm going to say that while it makes practical sense to examine social problems as objective (real, tangible) conditions involving real people, we can't stop there because it's *not enough*. Social problems are about things and people that we *worry* about and when we talk about "worry" we go beyond objectivity into the topic of *subjective definitions*. But you might ask, So what? Don't Americans worry about things we should worry about? Aren't experts qualified to tell us what we should worry about? To answer these questions we must leave the world of a common-sense practical actor in order to examine the confusions in this thing we're calling social problems. Let's look at why it's not good to simply assume that we worry about those things we should worry about.

Objective Characteristics and Subjective Worry

We can't simply assume that we worry about things we should worry about, because there is *no necessary relationship* between any objective indicators (statistics, results of tests) of social problem conditions and what Americans worry about, what politicians focus on, or what television, newspapers, or magazines present to us. This means there's no necessary relationship between the measurable characteristics of any given condition or the people in it and a definition of that condition as troublesome. So, sometimes Americans start to worry about a condition when objective indicators could be used to show that the *condition is not new*. For example, the historical record (an objective indicator) shows that what we now call "child abuse" always has been a part of human existence. Indeed, I could make a case that children in the past were much more likely to be brutally treated by their parents than are children now. Yet the term "child abuse" didn't appear in the United States until the 1960s. Or, how long did slavery exist before it was called a social problem? In these examples, objective indicators about the troublesome nature of conditions were available long before there was any worry about them. This means that we might not worry about something at one time and then start to worry about it at another time. Likewise, Americans can begin to worry about something when objective indicators could be used to show that the condition is actually *getting better.* For example, concern about "poverty" in this country comes and goes. In the most recent cycle of concern, politicians started talking about poverty as a problem in the 1960s. But this was when objective indicators were showing that the rates of poverty were declining rather than increasing. In this instance, a social problem was defined when (objectively speaking) the condition was getting better. Or, we can begin to worry about something when *there is no objective indicator* pointing to the presence of a prevalent condition. For example, the problem of crack cocaine entered public consciousness before there were any statistics indicating that its use was widespread; fear about the safety of children trick-or-treating on Halloween is based on very few incidents.

My point here is simple: there isn't always a neat and tidy relationship between objective indicators and what Americans worry about. We can worry when a widespread condition doesn't exist; we can have indicators of a troublesome condition and not worry about it.

There are responses to my point from people who believe that social problems should be studied as real conditions in the environment and that these conditions can be scientifically measured. First, these folks believe that it is the experts who really know when a social problem exists. When indicators show there is a prevalent, troublesome condition although the public isn't concerned, such experts call the condition a *latent social problem.* Latent means it's there, even if the public doesn't know it or doesn't worry about it. Or, when a public labels a condition a social problem but the objective indicators don't support this definition, experts argue that the problem is spurious— it's not real. In this view, social problems are about objective conditions and it doesn't really matter how those conditions are defined. We have a social problem (even if it's unrecognized) when objective indicators show we do; we don't have a social problem when objective indicators say one isn't there (even if many members of the public believe one exists).

Objective Characteristics and Cultural Fragmentation

If there isn't a necessary relationship between what people think is a problem and what really exists in the social world then perhaps the answer is to rely on experts to tell us what we should worry about. Would that resolve the trouble of differences between objective conditions and subjective definitions of these conditions as social problems? I don't think it would. I'd argue we can't get around the importance of subjective definitions because social problems are about morality. To name any condition a social problem is to take a moral stand—it's to believe that the condition is *wrong* and must be changed. So, we must go into the realm of the subjective and here we find *political, social,* and *moral fragmentation.*

I want to call your attention to a characteristic of my presentation so far. Repeatedly, I've defined social problems in terms such as things Americans worry about, or what we consider troublesome. But what do I mean when I say "Americans"? Who is this "we" I write about? To decide that a condition is a social problem is to take a moral stand (it's wrong, it needs fixing), but "we" are not a nation of people who agree with one another. Who has the power to say that one or another condition is wrong? Wrong for whom? Wrong for what reason? These are complex matters.

Academics often use the term *postmodern* to describe the characteristics of the United States (indeed, the world) as we are about to enter a new century. This is an important term for the study of social problems because it encourages us to be aware that we live in a time of political, social, and moral *fragmentation.* Fragmentation is the commonsense meaning of the term: It's about divisions, about splintering. So, for example, the postmodern is about *political fragmentation.* Loyalty to specific political parties doesn't matter much because few people follow the past tendency to vote "straight tickets." Americans now routinely vote for a president from one party and senators and representatives from another. So, too, terms such as liberal or conservative, left, or right, are relatively meaningless. It's primarily only politicians and other political experts who see the world through full-blown political belief systems (called *ideologies*). Most of us think about issues one at a time and it's not all that uncommon for us to hold very different views on different issues. Often the views we hold can be downright contradictory—some feminists agree with religious fundamentalists that "pornography" is a social problem that must be eradicated. Certainly these folks don't agree on much else.

There's also *social fragmentation*. We no longer are a nation of farmers more or less sharing similar experiences in life. We increasingly are *heterogeneous* (different) in our experiences. What experiences in life likely are shared by a young, unemployed Black man living in an inner-city ghetto and a wealthy, elderly White woman living in the suburbs? . . . What about people who are very religious (but of what religion you might ask because there are many) and those who aren't religious at all? What about people who trace their ancestry to the earliest immigrants to the United States in the 1600s and those newly arrived here (but from what country you might ask because not all immigrants are the same). Do we all experience the world in the same ways? Of course not.

This takes me to what social fragmentation means for the study of social problems. A basic sociological belief is that our experiences shape how we see the world. Social fragmentation leads to *moral fragmentation*. We live in a time when it's common for many Americans to resist making moral judgments. Moral decisions for these folks aren't grounded in any set of moral beliefs; morality simply depends. Yet we also live in a country where many others have a morality firmly grounded in religious belief. How, then, can we claim that any given condition necessarily is troublesome? Troublesome because of what? There isn't an easy answer.

A difficulty with assuming that social problems can be understood only as objective conditions in the social environment is that moral judgments are *necessary* to name something as a social problem. Such judgments can't be avoided because, by definition, a social problem is a condition defined as troublesome and in need of change. To say this is to take a moral stand and moral stands aren't objective.

Objective indicators can tell us what "is," they can't tell us what's "wrong." The problem of social and moral fragmentation leads to a question: Whose values lead to deciding that a particular condition is wrong and needs fixing?

Objective Characteristics and Knowledge

When social problems are studied as objective conditions, we rely on knowledge of these conditions to chart our actions toward them. But our postmodern world is a *mediated* world. Mediated means "through the media." How do we know what we know? Our world keeps getting bigger, more complex, and more confusing. Because each one of us can directly experience very little (about the world in general, about social problem conditions and the people in them in particular), we must rely on others to tell us. We often rely on the media for this information but this media tends to blur differences between fact and fiction, truth and fantasy When you watch an "infomercial" are you receiving information (factual) or a commercial (biased)? Is a "docudrama" a documentary (implying true) or a drama (implying fiction)? Where is the knowledge on "America's Most Wanted," a program blending actual (real) videotapes of a crime with reenactments (fiction) of the crime? Do real courts work like "People's Court" or "Dr. Ruth's Court"? Such are the problems of knowledge in our world.

Of course, those who believe we should study social problems as objective conditions would argue that we can't know the truth from the mediated world but that truth is knowable through science. Often this is true, but not always. We live in a time when experts of all types are routinely accused of being not so objective. Practical actors know that science can't always be trusted; we know that all too many experts can be paid to tell whatever story they're paid to tell. We've seen it on television: experts testifying on behalf of O.J. Simpson's innocence were followed by other experts who just as convincingly testified on behalf of his guilt. Scientific evidence is often piled high by each side, but this evidence is contradictory. What do we believe?

And what do we believe when experts keep changing their minds? What do we believe when we are told that scientific research shows cars now are much safer because of airbags but other scientific research tells us these same airbags kill children? . . . The scientific experts don't agree in the first place and they keep changing their minds in the second place.

At times, experts who change their minds can encourage major changes in the ways we think about social problems. For example, . . . in June 1998, the National Heart, Lung, and Blood Institute lowered by five pounds the official standard for being "overweight." Millions of people who weren't overweight suddenly were officially overweight so the problem now seems far worse. On the other hand, the problem of "educational failure" was instantly downgraded when professionals decided to recalculate SAT (Scholastic Aptitude Test) scores. By adding over one hundred points to each student's test, thousands of "low-achieving" students instantly were not so low-achieving. This is a problem of knowledge in our world.

. . . What I am arguing is that we shouldn't simply assume that objectivity or truthfulness flow naturally and automatically from science and research. Also as clearly and most certainly, I'm not trying to tell you that we can't or shouldn't study social problems as objective conditions in the social environment. Such study reflects the interests of practical actors interested in doing something about social problems and that is an important task. But what I *am* arguing is that if we confine ourselves to looking at social problems only as objective characteristics of our social environment we will miss other important issues. These are the many questions surrounding the definitional side of social problems. I'll begin with a brief introduction to a social construction perspective.

⊛ The Social Construction of Social Life and Social Problems

Social construction perspectives on social problems are an application of the general social construction theoretical perspective. . . . I will lay out in simple form the most basic points in this framework so that we can get on to the major topic of what kinds of questions it leads us to ask about social problems.

Humans Live in Two Worlds: The Physical World and the World of Meaning. Remember that the objective condition approach to social problems leads us to focus on the very real, tangible physical world inhabited by humans. We do live in this physical world. In my immediate environment at this moment my eyes see a desk, a computer, a clock, some bills to be paid, two cats, and so on. These are very real objects. But a social construction perspective is less concerned with the physical world than it is with how we *understand* this world. If I were a member of another culture I might look at my desk and understand it as firewood for cooking dinner; I might look at my cats and see what to cook for that dinner; I might look at my computer and see the workings of Satan. For the clock on my wall to be meaningful, I must have a concept of time and this concept must be one where minutes (rather than merely night and day) are important, and so on. Social construction perspectives aren't concerned with the objective world. Think of this as an academic division-of-labor: We'll let others concern themselves with the objective world. Social constructionism examines the *meaning* humans create in our world.

Social construction perspectives are concerned with social problems as *subjective definitions.* So, for example, we might be able to measure the number of calories people eat and medical science might be able to tell us whether or not this is enough for good health. We might then have an objective condition called "people not eating enough calories for good health." But this isn't enough to make this into a social problem. For there to be a social problem we first need to make sense of this condition. What is it? Is it unavoidable hunger, or religious fasting, or anorexia, or an eating fad? Then, we must attach a particular meaning (troublesome) to this condition. To do this takes moral reasoning: Why is it troublesome? Any objective condition can't be a social problem until it's named and given meaning. This is why it's possible to argue that a *social problem doesn't exist until it is defined as such.* Conditions might exist, people might be hurt by them, but they aren't social problems until humans categorize them as troublesome and in need of repair.

We React to the World and its Social Problems Through Our Meanings. Social construction perspectives are about more than how we categorize the objects and people in our world. They go on to argue that our categorizations *influence our behaviors.* So, for example, I have named my two cats (Mel and Ella). They reign as king and queen of my household. I can predict with utmost certainty that I won't eat them for dinner tonight. While in the physical world, cats (as well as dogs and grubs) are (objectively speaking) nutritious human foods, the meaning I've attached to the physical category of "cats" makes it impossible for me in my normal daily life to think of them as food. Humans react toward objects in terms of the meaning we give these objects.

What this means for the study of social problems is that it's important to know *how* we give meaning to objects in our environment because those meanings will encourage us to react toward those objects in particular ways. Consider . . . the two sides of the debate about abortion. Objectively speaking, abortion is a medical procedure; it doesn't have any necessary meaning. Yet the social problem of "abortion" certainly is a problem of meaning. But what kind of meaning? One side of the debate about this medical procedure has chosen the label "pro-life," which encourages us to think of this medical procedure in terms of the fetus. The other side has chosen the name "pro-choice," which encourages us to think of this *same* procedure in terms of women. The same condition can be given different meanings, and these different meanings encourage us to have different reactions. Social construction perspectives examine these meanings.

As a quick side note, have you yet noticed my tendency to use quotation marks around many words? If you haven't yet, you eventually will and this will tend to wear on your nerves because the quotation marks will cause you to pause for just a moment. I apologize, but this is my intent. When I put quotation marks around a word such as "pro-choice," I want to call your attention to the *word* itself. I want you to stop for a very short moment and ask yourself, What is this? In daily life, we rarely ask one another to define words we are using. We use words such as "poverty" or "drug pusher" without thinking. Constructionist perspectives encourage us to take words seriously because even the most simple words (*particularly* the most simple words) are categories for entire systems of meaning. To take an example of how words matter, consider that public support is much stronger for "spending taxpayers' money on food programs for low-income families" than it is for "spending taxpayers' money on Food Stamp programs." Same activity, but different words have different meanings.

We Understand Our World and its Social Problems Through Our Categorizations. Part of the experience of all humans is that we *categorize*. The names we attach to objects in our world are labels for types of things or types of people. So, although each of my two cats is unique, both are members of the category of "cats" (as are lions and tigers at the zoo). In daily life we see similarities among diversity. We talk about "crime" as if it were a thing, but crime includes not buckling your seat belt as well as mass murder; we categorize people in categories such as gender (women, men), race/ethnicity (Asian, African, Anglo, Hispanic, etc.), age (baby, child, teen, etc.), economic class (poor, middle-class, rich), and on and on. A primary characteristic of the way we understand our world is that we categorize.

In daily life our commonsense categories serve us well. Indeed, they serve us so well that once we learn them in childhood (children must be taught what food is—and what it isn't; they learn to distinguish women from men and so on), we don't need to think about them. Only when we travel to a far different culture can we see that our categories and their particular contents are matters of *human definition* that don't flow necessarily from physical objects. This means that the categories and their contents are *socially constructed,* and this raises all kinds of questions: What objects go in what categories? What are the meanings of the categories themselves?

The term "social problems" is a name for a category. I think of a name such as "social problems" as a *label;* I think of categories as *containers.* In the metaphor of categories as containers, the label "social problems" is on a container that holds those conditions Americans believe are widespread, wrong, changeable, and in need of change. Because like all categories it is socially constructed rather than flowing necessarily from the objects placed into it, we can ask questions about the category. Art critics often ask: "What is art?" We can ask: "What is a social problem?" More specifically, we can ask what is "crime," or what is "environmental ruin," or what is "racism." We can ask who are "criminals," or "racists," or "sexually abused children." The meanings of each of these goes far beyond the name on the container. For example, one social problems textbook defines "racism" as "A belief in the superiority of one racial group over another that leads to prejudice and discrimination."[2] To that, I say, fine, but then I want to ask: What is a "racial group"? What is "prejudice"? What is "discrimination"? How do we know these things when we see them? What kinds of behaviors and people are included and which aren't? "Racism" is a label on a container but that doesn't tell us a great deal. Social construction perspectives encourage us to look more closely.

We Understand the Categories in Our World Through Typifications. Humans categorize conditions and people. But when we think about this, there are two characteristics of the social world that make this a very complicated process.

First, each category is held together by an organizing device (what I'll call a *frame*). To begin simply, the category food contains "things to eat." This means the category food contains liver and chocolate cake, pigs feet and caviar. These are very different things sharing only the commonality that they are "things to eat." This becomes more complicated when we get to our categorizations of people: We categorize half the world's population as "women," and the other half as "men." While in daily life we most often do this (and uncountable other categorizations) without thinking, if you do think about it for just a moment, it's amazing: What are we looking at when we do these categorizations? And, just as important, what are we ignoring in order to see similarities? The first complexity in understanding our world in terms of categories is that this requires us to see *similarities* among incredibly diverse objects.

The second complexity of understanding our world in terms of categories comes from what I called the postmodern condition: Our world is altogether too big and complex for us to experience it all. Granted, some of our images come from our own experiences: If we have a painful experience the first time we go to a dentist, we might form an image of "dentistry" as painful—even if it's not so painful for most people most of the time. If you happen to have a woman (man, Black, White, elderly, young) boss who's kind (terrible) you might form an image of this *kind* (category) of person as this *kind* (category) of boss. But obviously, because our own experiences are so limited, our images based on practical experiences won't get us very far. Most of us don't experience social problem conditions firsthand; these conditions aren't a part of our lived reality. And even if we do personally experience a social problem condition, we have only our own experience and this personal experience might be far different from the experience of others.

In the distant past, people could enlarge their own experiences only by talking with friends and family, so their worlds tended to remain small. By the last century, printed books, magazines, and newspapers became widely available and these greatly expanded the possibilities of having images of conditions and people that weren't from personal experience. Now, of course, we live in a world where radio, movies, television, and the World Wide Web can greatly enlarge our experiences. Think about what you know about the world; think about how little of what you know comes from what you have directly experienced.

So humans categorize and we often do this not based on our personal experience. This leads me to the point: We categorize by *typification*. Think of a typification as a picture in our heads of typical kinds of things, be these "cats" or "abused children" or "ecological ruin." Because we can't know all cats, abused children, or instances of environmental ruin, we have an image of the typical.

My students often stop me at this point and complain that what I'm calling an image or a typification is really nothing other than a *stereotype*. In one way, they're right: the concepts of typification and stereotype have very similar formal meanings. All are about preexisting images of types of things or types of people. And none include much room for emphasizing the many ways that each thing or person is different from all others. But it's still not right to say that a typification is the same as a stereotype. This is because the term *stereotype* has drifted into popular culture and now has a very narrow meaning. . . . We say, "You're stereotyping," when we believe others are denying complexity. . . . We say, "That's just a stereotype," when we believe the preexisting typification doesn't match the objective reality. But from a social construction perspective the issue is far more complex, because we begin with the understanding that *we have no choice* but to use typifications. For example, when I say "AIDS," what comes into your mind? What mental picture do you have? Did you think, "I have no image" or "Each case of AIDS is different"? Maybe, but my hunch is that most readers have at least a vague image of AIDS. If you do then I would ask you how much of this mental picture is based on your own personal experience and how much of your image has come from what you've heard others say, from what you've read, from what you've seen on television or in movies such as *Philadelphia*. Even if you are an AIDS activist, even if you live in a community devastated by AIDS, you can personally know only a very limited number of people affected by AIDS. Most of what you know is a typification. . . .

My point is that our world is altogether too big and complex for us to refuse to use typifications. We *cannot* know the individuality of each and every thing, condition, and person in our world. So, while the term stereotype is associated with only negative consequences, the terms of typification or image should be understood as *social resources* to help us get through our days. While we will see as we go along that using typifications *can* have very negative consequences, typifications also can have very positive consequences. After all, the only feeling we can have about events we don't personally experience and about people we don't personally know is through our typifications. Without these pictures in our heads we wouldn't be able to understand other than our own extremely limited personal experience. Without these pictures in our heads we wouldn't know how to react to the countless others in the world of strangers we encounter daily. I can feel sorry for "crack babies" even though I've never personally seen one; I can think about extreme poverty even though I don't live in it; I can talk to my students about prisons and jails even though none of us have ever been confined in one. Without typifications, we could only think and feel about things that we had actually experienced. Without typifications, our worlds would be very small.

Typifications are important in social problems. Because each of us experiences so little of life's possibilities, we must rely on our images. Rather than merely condemn their (mis)use, constructionist perspectives examine *how* and why typifications come into being, they explore their *use* by humans.

This has been an extremely brief tour through some of the major points of social construction perspectives that obviously are important to studying the definitional side of social problems. The major point is that this framework is concerned first, foremost, and primarily with the *subjective definition* of social problems.

. . .

⊌ An Invitation to Social Construction Perspectives on Social Problems

From the perspective of practical actors concerned with doing something about social problems, social construction perspectives might seem to focus on trivial questions. In daily life, it seems that what's important is the very real human suffering caused by social problems as real conditions in the social environment; it doesn't seem important to ask how we know what we know.

To this I would reply, Yes, there are many conditions that create human suffering and we need to know about these conditions; we need to know about the people who do this harm; we need to know about the people who experience this harm. I also would reply that I don't believe that looking at the construction of social problems means we have to deny or discount social problems as objective conditions. I'm *not* asking you to forget that poverty, crime, AIDS, racism, and so on are very real in their consequences. But I also *do* believe that questions raised by social construction perspectives are anything but trivial and that to ignore these questions leads to a less than complete understanding of social problems. Here I invite you to consider some of these questions: Why is it that some conditions—and not others—become the focus of public attention? What kinds of claims likely will be successful in leading to social change? What are the relationships between successful social problems claims and our practical efforts to do something about troublesome conditions and the people in them? How can what we think about the world change the world in very real ways? I'd like to encourage you to think about what you know about the world and about how you know it. I want you to think about this because, in the final analysis, what can be done about social problems depends on who wins—and who loses—the social problems game.

ℰndnotes

[1]The distinction between "personal trouble" and "social issue" was made by C. Wright Mills: "Troubles occur within the character of the individual and within the range of his immediate relations with others. . . . Issues have to do with matters that transcend these local environments of the individual and the range of his inner life" (1959:8).

[2]James Coleman and Donald Cressey (1996:567).

𝓡eferences

Mills, C. Wright (1959). *The Sociological Imagination*. New York: Oxford University Press.

◎ ◎ ◎

𝒬uestions

1. From the objective conditions perspective, what is a social problem? What are the questions one would ask about social problems from this perspective?

2. From the social construction perspective, what is a social problem? What are the questions one would ask about social problems from this perspective?

3. What are typifications? Why are they important in the study of social problems? Give an example to illustrate your answer.

4. Ask five people what they think are the three most serious social problems facing the world today. Record their answers and bring them to class. Collate and compare the answers you recorded to those reported by your classmates. How much similarity is there? How does this exercise help illustrate Loseke's point that social problems are about disagreements?

The Power Elite

C. WRIGHT MILLS

*There are many objective and putative (i.e., alleged or imag-
ined) conditions that are not treated as social problems by
those that C. Wright Mills called the "power elite." The power
elite do not use their social positions, power, and connections
to define particular conditions as social problems because they
do not experience these conditions as problematic. As you read
this piece, think about why the power elite might define social
problems differently than you do.*

Except for the unsuccessful Civil War, changes in the power system of the United States have not involved important challenges to its basic legitimations. Even when they have been decisive
enough to be called "revolutions," they have not involved the "resort
to the guns of a cruiser, the dispersal of an elected assembly by bay-
onets, or the mechanisms of a police state."[1] Nor have they involved,
in any decisive way, any ideological struggle to control masses.
Changes in the American structure of power have generally come
about by institutional shifts in the relative positions of the political,
the economic, and the military orders.

. . .

The Nature of the Power Elite

We study history, it has been said, to rid ourselves of it, and the history of the power elite is a clear case for which this maxim is correct.
Like the tempo of American life in general, the long-term trends of
the power structure have been greatly speeded up since World War

---

"The Power Elite," by C. Wright Mills, reprinted from *The Power Elite*, 1956.
Copyright © by Oxford University Press. pp. 269–297.

II, and certain newer trends within and between the dominant institutions have also set the shape of the power elite. . . .

I. In so far as the structural clue to the power elite today lies in the political order, that clue is the decline of politics as genuine and public debate of alternative decisions—with nationally responsible and policy-coherent parties and with autonomous organizations connecting the lower and middle levels of power with the top levels of decision. America is now in considerable part more a formal political democracy than a democratic social structure, and even the formal political mechanics are weak.

The long-time tendency of business and government to become more intricately and deeply involved with each other has, in the fifth epoch, reached a new point of explicitness. The two cannot now be seen clearly as two distinct worlds. It is in terms of the executive agencies of the state that the rapprochement has proceeded most decisively. The growth of the executive branch of the government, with its agencies that patrol the complex economy, does not mean merely the "enlargement of government" as some sort of autonomous bureaucracy: it has meant the ascendancy of the corporation's man as a political eminence. . . .

II. In so far as the structural clue to the power elite today lies in the enlarged and military state, that clue becomes evident in the military ascendancy. The warlords have gained decisive political relevance, and the military structure of America is now in considerable part a political structure. The seemingly permanent military threat places a premium on the military and upon their control of men, material, money, and power; virtually all political and economic actions are now judged in terms of military definitions of reality: the higher warlords have ascended to a firm position within the power elite of the fifth epoch. . . .

III. In so far as the structural clue to the power elite today lies in the economic order, that clue is the fact that the economy is at once a permanent-war economy and a private-corporation economy. American capitalism is now in considerable part a military capitalism, and the most important relation of the big corporation to the state rests on the coincidence of interests between military and corporate needs, as defined by warlords and corporate rich. Within the elite as a whole, this coincidence of interest between the high military and the corporate chieftains strengthens both of them and further subordinates the role of the merely political men. Not politicians, but corporate executives, sit with the military and plan the organization of war effort. . . .

The power elite is composed of political, economic, and military men, but this instituted elite is frequently in some tension: it comes together only on certain coinciding points and only on certain occasions of "crisis." In the long peace of the nineteenth century, the military were not in the high councils of state, not of the political directorate, and neither were the economic men—they made raids upon the state but they did not join its directorate. During the 'thirties, the political man was ascendant. Now the military and the corporate men are in top positions.

Of the three types of circle that compose the power elite today, it is the military that has benefited the most in its enhanced power, although the corporate circles have also become more explicitly entrenched in the more public decision-making circles. It is the professional politician that has lost the most, so much that in examining the events and decisions, one is tempted to speak of a political vacuum in which the corporate rich and the high warlord, in their coinciding interest, rule.

It should not be said that the three "take turns" in carrying the initiative, for the mechanics of the power elite are not often as deliberate as that would imply. At times, of course, it is—as when political men, thinking they can borrow the prestige of generals, find that they must pay for it, or, as when during big slumps, economic men feel the need of a politician at once safe and possessing vote appeal. Today all three are involved in virtually all widely ramifying decisions. Which of the three types seems to lead depends upon "the tasks of the period" as they, the elite, define them. Just now, these tasks center upon "defense" and international affairs. Accordingly, as we have seen, the military are ascendant in two senses: as personnel and as

41

justifying ideology. That is why, just now, we can most easily specify the unity and the shape of the power elite in terms of the military ascendancy.

But we must always be historically specific and open to complexities. The simple Marxian view makes the big economic man the *real* holder of power; the simple liberal view makes the big political man the chief of the power system; and there are some who would view the warlords as virtual dictators. Each of these is an oversimplified view. It is to avoid them that we use the term "power elite" rather than, for example, "ruling class."

In so far as the power elite has come to wide public attention, it has done so in terms of "military clique." The power elite does, in fact, take its current shape from the decisive entrance into it of the military. Their presence and their ideology are its major legitimations, whenever the power elite feels the need to provide any. But what is called the "Washington military clique" is not composed merely of military men, and it does not prevail merely in Washington. Its members exist all over the country, and it is a coalition of generals in the roles of corporation executives, of politicians masquerading as admirals, of corporation executives acting like politicians, of civil servants who become majors, of vice-admirals who are also the assistants to a cabinet officer, who is himself, by the way, really a member of the managerial elite.

Neither the idea of a "ruling class" nor of a simple monolithic rise of "bureaucratic politicians" nor of a "military clique" is adequate. The power elite today involves the often uneasy coincidence of economic, military, and political power.

· · ·

☻ The Composition of the Power Elite

Despite their social similarity and psychological affinities, the members of the power elite do not constitute a club having a permanent membership with fixed and formal boundaries. It is of the nature of the power elite that within it there is a good deal of shifting about, and that it thus does not consist of one small set of the same men in the same positions in the same hierarchies. Because men know each other personally does not mean that among them there is a unity of policy; and because they do not know each other personally does not mean that among them there is a disunity. The conception of the power elite does not rest, as I have repeatedly said, primarily upon personal friendship.

As the requirements of the top places in each of the major hierarchies become similar, the types of men occupying these roles at the top—by selection and by training in the jobs—become similar. This is no mere deduction from structure to personnel. That it is a fact is revealed by the heavy traffic that has been going on between the three structures, often in very intricate patterns. The chief executives, the warlords, and selected politicians came into contact with one another in an intimate, working way during World War II; after that war ended, they continued their associations, out of common beliefs, social congeniality, and coinciding interests. Noticeable proportions of top men from the military, the economic, and the political worlds have during the last fifteen years occupied positions in one or both of the other worlds: between these higher circles there is an interchangeability of position based formally upon the supposed transferability of "executive ability," based in substance upon the co-optation by cliques of insiders. As members of a power elite, many of those busy in this traffic have come to look upon "the government" as an umbrella under whose authority they do their work.

As the business between the big three increases in volume and importance, so does the traffic in personnel. The very criteria for selecting men who will rise come to embody this fact. The corporate commissar, dealing with the state and its military, is wiser to choose a young man who has experienced the state and its military than one who has not. The political director, often dependent for his own political success upon corporate decisions and corporations, is also wiser to choose a man with corporate experience. Thus, by virtue of the very criterion of success, the interchange of personnel and the unity of the power elite is increased.

Given the formal similarity of the three hierarchies in which the several members of the elite spend their working lives, given the ramifications of the decisions made in each upon the others, given the coincidence of interest that prevails among them at many points, and given the administrative vacuum of the American civilian state along with its enlargement of tasks—given these trends of structure, and adding to them the psychological affinities we have noted—we should indeed be surprised were we to find that men said to be skilled in administrative contacts and full of organizing ability would fail to do more than get in touch with one another. They have, of course, done much more than that: increasingly, they assume positions in one another's domains.

The unity revealed by the interchangeability of top roles rests upon the parallel development of the top jobs in each of the big three domains. The interchange occurs most frequently at the points of their coinciding interest, as between regulatory agency and the regulated industry; contracting agency and contractor. And, as we shall see, it leads to co-ordinations that are more explicit, and even formal.

The inner core of the power elite consists, first, of those who interchange commanding roles at the top of one dominant institutional order with those in another: the admiral who is also a banker and a lawyer and who heads up an important federal commission; the corporation executive whose company was one of the two or three leading war material producers who is now the Secretary of Defense; the wartime general who dons civilian clothes to sit on the political directorate and then becomes a member of the board of directors of a leading economic corporation.

Although the executive who becomes a general, the general who becomes a statesman, the statesman who becomes a banker, see much more than ordinary men in their ordinary environments, still the perspectives of even such men often remain tied to their dominant locales. In their very career, however, they interchange roles within the big three and thus readily transcend the particularity of interest in any one of these institutional milieux. By their very careers and activities, they lace the three types of milieux together. They are, accordingly, the core members of the power elite.

These men are not necessarily familiar with every major arena of power. We refer to one man who moves in and between perhaps two circles—say the industrial and the military—and to another man who moves in the military and the political, and to a third who moves in the political as well as among opinion-makers. These in-between types most closely display our image of the power elite's structure and operation, even of behind-the-scenes operations. To the extent that there is any "invisible elite," these advisory and liaison types are its core. Even if—as I believe to be very likely—many of them are, at least in the first part of their careers, "agents" of the various elites rather than themselves elite, it is they who are most active in organizing the several top milieux into a structure of power and maintaining it.

· · ·

The outermost fringes of the power elite—which change more than its core—consist of "those who count" even though they may not be "in" on given decisions of consequence nor in their career move between the hierarchies. Each member of the power elite need not be a man who personally decides every decision that is to be ascribed to the power elite. Each member, in the decisions that he does make, takes the others seriously into account. They not only make decisions in the several major areas of war and peace; they are the men who, in decisions in which they take no direct part, are taken into decisive account by those who are directly in charge.

On the fringes and below them, somewhat to the side of the lower echelons, the power elite fades off into the middle levels of power, into the rank and file of the Congress, the pressure groups that are not vested in the power elite itself, as well as a multiplicity of regional and state and local interests. If all the men on the middle levels are not among those who count, they sometimes must be taken into account, handled, cajoled, broken or raised to higher circles.

· · ·

◉ The Interests of the Power Elite

The conception of the power elite and of its unity rests upon the corresponding developments and the coincidence of interests among economic, political, and military organizations. It also rests upon the similarity of origin and outlook, and the social and personal intermingling of the top circles from each of these dominant hierarchies. This conjunction of institutional and psychological forces, in turn, is revealed by the heavy personnel traffic within and between the big three institutional orders, as well as by the rise of go-betweens as in the high-level lobbying. The conception of the power elite, accordingly, does *not* rest upon the assumption that American history since the origins of World War II must be understood as a secret plot, or as a great and co-ordinated conspiracy of the members of this elite. The conception rests upon quite impersonal grounds.

There is, however, little doubt that the American power elite—which contains, we are told some of the greatest organizers in the world—has also planned and has plotted. The rise of the elite, as we have already made clear, was not and could not have been caused by a plot; and the tenability of the conception does not rest upon the existence of any secret or any publicly known organization. But, once the conjunction of structural trend and of the personal will to utilize it gave rise to the power elite, then plans and programs did occur to its members and indeed it is not possible to interpret many events and official policies of the fifth epoch without reference to the power elite. "There is a great difference," Richard Hofstadter has remarked, "between locating conspiracies in history and saying that history *is*, in effect, a conspiracy. . . . "

The structural trends of institutions become defined as opportunities by those who occupy their command posts. Once such opportunities are recognized, men may avail themselves of them. Certain types of men from each of the dominant institutional areas, more farsighted than others, have actively promoted the liaison before it took its truly modern shape. They have often done so for reasons not shared by their partners, although not objected to by them either; and often the outcome of their liaison has had consequences which none of them foresaw, much less shaped, and which only later in the course of development came under explicit control. Only after it was well under way did most of its members find themselves part of it and become gladdened, although sometimes also worried, by this fact. But once the co-ordination is a going concern, new men come readily into it and assume its existence without question.

So far as explicit organization—conspiratorial or not—is concerned, the power elite, by its very nature, is more likely to use existing organizations, working within and between them, than to set up explicit organizations whose membership is strictly limited to its own members. But if there is no machinery in existence to ensure for example, that military and political factors will be balanced in decisions made, they will invent such machinery and use it, as with the National Security Council. Moreover, in a formally democratic polity, the aims and the powers of the various elements of this elite are further supported by an aspect of the permanent war economy: the assumption that the security of the nation supposedly rests upon great secrecy of plan and intent. Many higher events that would reveal the working of the power elite can be withheld from public knowledge under the guise of secrecy. With the wide secrecy covering their operations and decisions, the power elite can mask their intentions, operations, and further consolidation. Any secrecy that is imposed upon those in positions to observe high decision-makers clearly works for and not against the operations of the power elite.

There is accordingly reason to suspect—but by the nature of case, no proof—that the power elite is not altogether "surfaced." There is nothing hidden about it, although its members often know one another, seem quite naturally to work together, and share many organizations in common. There is nothing conspiratorial about it, although its decisions are often publicly unknown and its mode of operation manipulative rather than explicit.

· · ·

◎ Conclusion

The idea of the power elite rests upon and enables us to make sense of (1) the decisive institutional trends that characterize the structure of our epoch, in particular, the military ascendancy in a privately incorporated economy, and more broadly, the several coincidences of objective interests between economic, military, and political institutions; (2) the social similarities and the psychological affinities of the men who occupy the command posts of these structures, in particular the increased interchangeability of the top positions in each of them and the increased traffic between these orders in the careers of men of power; (3) the ramifications, to the point of virtual totality, of the kind of decisions that are made at the top, and the rise to power of a set of men who, by training and bent, are professional organizers of considerable force and who are unrestrained by democratic party training.

Negatively, the formation of the power elite rests upon (1) the relegation of the professional party politician to the middle levels of power, (2) the semi-organized stalemate of the interests of sovereign localities into which the legislative function has fallen, (3) the virtually complete absence of a civil service that constitutes a politically neutral, but politically relevant, depository of brainpower and executive skill, and (4) the increased official secrecy behind which great decisions are made without benefit of public or even Congressional debate.

As a result, the political directorate, the corporate rich, and the ascendant military have come together as the power elite, and the expanded and centralized hierarchies which they head have encroached upon the old balances and have now relegated them to the middle levels of power. Now the balancing society is a conception that pertains accurately to the middle levels, and on that level the balance has become more often an affair of intrenched provincial and nationally irresponsible forces and demands than a center of power and national decision.

. . .

ℰndnote
[1]Hofstadter, R. op. cit., pp. 71–72.

❧ ❧ ❧

Questions

1. Define the power elite. According to Mills, which three domains or institutions make up the core of the power elite?

2. Of the three domains, which takes precedence? Explain the interplay among the three institutions. How do the interests of these three groups conflict? How are their interests similar?

3. To what degree does Mills rely on a "conspiracy theory" to explain the existence and continued prominence of the power elite?

4. Mills's thesis was first presented some four decades ago to explain a historical pattern that may or may not be applicable today. Which groups do you think make up the power elite in contemporary American society? Which groups constitute the power elite in other societies? Speculate as to why these groups might differ across cultures or societies.

5. How might the interests of the power elite influence what things we do or do not define as social problems? Explain.

Three Mile Island: A New Species of Trouble

KAI ERIKSON

In this selection, Kai Erikson examines the relationship between the accident at Three Mile Island nuclear power plant and local residents' response to the accident. In particular, Erikson explores the ways in which people tried to make sense of their situations. He concludes that this new species of troubles has altered the fundamental perceptions and fears that people have about their environment.

On the morning of March 28, 1979, one of two generating units at a little-known place called Three Mile Island experienced an odd sequence of equipment failures and human errors, resulting in the escape of several puffs of radioactive steam. It was a moment of considerable potential danger, as we all were soon to learn. And it was a moment of considerable uncertainty as well.

When the uncertainty was at its height, the governor of Pennsylvania issued a calm and measured advisory suggesting that pregnant women and preschool children living within a five-mile radius of the plant might want to evacuate, while others within a distance of ten miles ought to consider taking shelter in their own homes. In effect, the governor was recommending that 3,500 people living in the shadows of the reactor relocate for at least the immediate time being and that everyone else stay put.

Instead some 150,000 people were alarmed enough to take to the public highways, and they fled, on the average, a remarkable hundred miles. For every person advised to leave home, almost 45 did. This was not the largest evacuation in human history by any means, but it seems to have involved the widest imbalance on record between the scale of an advisory and the scale of an actual evacuation, and it involved the longest average flight as well.[1]

Three young geographers from Michigan State University called this "the evacuation shadow phenomenon," meaning by it the gap between what official wisdom called for and what the people at risk, acting on wisdoms of their own, actually did.[2] Specialists as well as laypeople often try to span that gap by stringing a makeshift term across it. "Overreaction" is much in vogue these days. So is "irrationality." But to describe the gap in that way after the fact is to give it a name without saying anything useful about it at all. The important questions to ask are: Of what did that shadow consist? What were the wisdoms on which the evacuees acted? And the best answer to both questions, clearly, is: a deep and profound dread.

The accident at Three Mile Island is a particularly instructive one since we know only in the most approximate way how much radiation was released or how much harm, if any, it did. So in one sense, at least, the feeling generated there was pure dread, perfect dread, the very essence of dread. It was not a reaction to anything the senses could apprehend: the smell of smoke, the sound of breaking timbers, the sting of burning eyes, the sight of falling bodies, or, in general, the contagious sense of alarm and excitement that erupts among people who share a time of danger. There was no panic, just quiet withdrawal over a number of hours. Each of those 150,000 (or at least the ones who made the decision to withdraw on behalf of other family members) was reacting to an individual reading of whatever portents could be found out there in a silent landscape.

What the evacuees feared in this instance, of course, was radiation, but it might well have been some other form of toxicity. I want to suggest, in fact, that radiation is but one strain of a whole new species of trouble that we are sure to see more of in years to come. Recent events at Three Mile Island and Chernobyl, say, both of them involving radiation, are of a kind with recent events at Love Canal and Bhopal, both of them involving toxic substances of another sort. And they are of a kind with the mercury spill that visited Grassy Narrows as well as the gasoline spill that worked its way into the ground under East Swallow.

The first thing to say about this new species of trouble . . . is that it is a product of human hands.

The ancients feared pestilence, drought, famine, flood, plague, and all the other scourges that darken the pages of the Bible. These miseries trouble us yet, to be sure, but it is fair to say that we have learned ways to defend ourselves against many of the worst of them. Some (certain epidemics, for example) can now be arrested or even prevented altogether. Others (hurricanes, tidal waves) can be seen far enough in advance for people to move out of their path, thus neutralizing much of their lethal force.

The irony, though, is that the technological advances that have afforded us this degree of protection from natural disasters have created a whole new category of events that specialists have come to call technological disasters—meaning everything that can go wrong when systems fail, humans err, designs prove faulty, engines misfire, and so on. Earthquakes, floods, hurricanes, volcanic eruptions, and tidal waves would be classed as "natural"; collisions, explosions, breakdowns, collapses, and, of course, crises like the ones at Chernobyl and Bhopal, . . . and East Swallow, belong on the roster of the "technological."

Technological disasters have clearly grown in number as we humans test the outer limits of our competence, but more to the point, they have also grown in scale. This is true in the sense that events of local origin can have consequences that reach across huge distances, as was the case, say, with Chernobyl. It is also true in the sense that news of it is broadcast so quickly and so widely that it becomes a moment in everyone's history, a datum in everyone's store of knowledge, a part of our collective consciousness, as was the case with Three Mile Island.

The distinction between natural and technological disasters is sometimes hard to draw exactly. When a mine shaft collapses in Appalachia, it is often a collaboration of restless mountain and careless people; when an epidemic spreads across Central Africa, it owes its virulence to both tough new strains of bacillus and stubborn old human habits.

However hard it may be to draw in actuality, though, that line usually seems distinct enough to victims. Natural disasters are almost always experienced as acts of God or caprices of nature. They happen *to* us. They *visit* us, as if from afar. Technological disasters, however, being of human manufacture, are at least in principle preventable, so there is always a story to be told about them, always a moral to be drawn from them, always a share of blame to be assigned. It is almost impossible to imagine a commission of inquiry, called to discover the causes of some dreadful calamity, concluding simply that it "just happened." We look for responsible human agents, and we find them. . . .

Now there is a sense in which it *did* "just happen." This is not because the fates are full of mischief sometimes but because accidents are simply bound to happen sooner or later as human systems become more and more elaborate. When geologists describe a floodplain as being of the kind that is likely to be inundated once in every fifty years, they are not using a logic all that different from that of engineers who describe a core melt as the kind of disturbance that is likely to happen once in every twenty thousand reactor years of operation. The flood is an act of God; the core melt, a human mistake. But both have been written into a kind of script. Both are "natural" in the sense of being foreseeable, even inevitable. The flood lies beyond our control, we say, because nature is simply like that. But core melts can also be described as beyond our control because human systems, too, are simply like that. We know in advance that hands will slip and machinery fail some predictable fraction of the time. This makes of them what Charles Perrow calls "normal accidents."[3]

Technological accidents, though, are almost never understood as the way the world of chance sorts itself out. They provoke outrage rather than acceptance or resignation. They generate a feeling that the thing ought not have happened, that someone is at fault, that victims deserve not only compassion and compensation but something akin to what lawyers call punitive damages. This feeling can become an absorbing passion for survivors and, for some, almost a way of life. To understand the feelings and reactions that technological emergencies provoke, then, it is crucial to distinguish the crises that are seen as the work of nature from those that are seen as the work of humankind. . . .

The second thing to be said about these new troubles is that they involve toxins: They contaminate rather than merely damage; they pollute, befoul, and taint rather than just create wreckage; they penetrate human tissue indirectly rather than wound the surfaces by assaults of a more straightforward kind.[4] And the evidence is growing that they scare human beings in new and special ways, that they elicit an uncanny fear in us. One of the surest findings to emerge from the new field of risk assessment is that people in general find radiation and other toxic substances a good deal more threatening than natural hazards of virtually any kind and technological hazards of considerable danger that do not involve toxicity.[5]

Example: The incident at Three Mile Island gave rise to a round of discussions about evacuation plans at other nuclear power plants, among them the Shoreham Nuclear Power Station on Long Island. In the course of that debate Suffolk County officials commissioned a survey to ask Long Island residents how they would react to a mishap at Shoreham. If an accident occurred, one question read, and everyone living within five miles of the plant were advised to stay indoors, what would you do? More than 40% of the residents living within a ten-mile radius of the reactor—together with 25% of the entire population of Long Island!—announced they would flee. And if pregnant women and young children were advised to evacuate? Then 55% of the people within ten miles and more than a third of the total Long Island population would leave. These are the mildest advisories that can be issued, and the latter, of course, was the one broadcast at Three Mile Island. More urgent ones, the survey indicated, would swell the number of evacuees still further, adding to the severity of what would already be utter deadlock.[6]

These are expressions of *intention,* it is important to note, and not reports of actual *behavior,* so they need to be viewed with the usual caution. But the percentage of people who expect to evacuate Long Island and the percentage of those who did in fact evacuate the neighborhood of Three Mile Island are nearly equal, and that degree of corroboration compels an additional measure of respect.

To throw a more recent log onto that small but sturdy fire, telephone surveys done in response to the government's proposal to build a high-level nuclear waste repository at Yucca Mountain in Nevada only confirm what other readings of the human mood have revealed: that people in general have an uncommon dread of things nuclear.[7]

• • •

Most technical experts seem to assume that increased experience and familiarity will act over time to reduce the dread and sense of mystery. Those feelings seem entirely illogical after all: Fifty thousand persons are killed every year in traffic accidents without provoking any deep aversion to automobiles, so why should we be so afraid of nuclear power plants and toxic waste dumps, which, on their face, do much less damage? This thought encourages a hope on the part of some experts that people will one day become as resigned and philosophical about radiological accidents as they are now about hurricanes or earthquakes. One of the most thoughtful pronuclear physicists has noted how much easier it is to "scare" people than to "unscare" them, but his reading of human history has persuaded him that people will sooner or later overcome this apprehension as they did their initial fears of electricity.[8] . . .

But why should toxic crises create so much alarm? What makes them seem so different? . . . In seeking some answers to those questions, I will be calling on the voices of a handful of people who lived through the emergency at Three Mile Island. The voices are those of plaintiffs in a legal action speaking several years after the event itself, so we have no right to assume that they represent the feelings of

everyone in the neighborhood. We do know, however, that the out-
looks expressed here are widely shared at Three Mile Island and,
moreover, that they are common to other places studied by social scientists where toxic contamination has struck.[9]

One reason toxic emergencies provoke such concern is that they
are not bounded, that they have no frame. We generally use the word
"disaster" in everyday conversation to refer to a distinct event that
interrupts the accustomed flow of everyday life. "Disasters" seem to
adhere to Aristotle's rules of drama. They have "a beginning and a
middle and an end." They "do not begin and end at random." They
have "a certain magnitude" yet are "easily taken in by the eye." They
have *plot,* in short, which is "the first principle and as it were the soul
of tragedy."[10]

An alarm sounds the beginning. It is a signal to retreat, to take to
storm cellars, to move to higher ground, to crouch in the shelter of
whatever cover presents itself. A period of destruction then follows
that may take no more than a brief, shattering moment or may last
many days. Sooner or later, though, the disaster comes to an exhaust-
ed close. The floodwaters recede, the smoke clears, the winds abate,
the bombers leave, and an all clear is sounded either literally or figu-
ratively. An announcement is then heard that the emergency is over
and that the time is now at hand for cleaning up and restoration. The
time has also come for that extraordinary moment when a fire marshal or a sheriff or whoever is in charge of such ceremonies casts a
shrewd eye over the devastation and estimates for the press how
many dollars of property damage was done. The pain may last, of
course; dreams may continue to haunt and wounds prove difficult to
heal. But the event itself is over, and what follows will be described
as "aftermath." "In the wake of the flood," we will say.

Toxic disasters, however, violate all the rules of plot. Some of
them have clearly defined beginnings, such as the explosion that sig-
naled the emergency at Chernobyl or the sudden moment of realiza-
tion that opened the drama of Bhopal; others begin long years before
anyone senses that something is wrong, as was the case at Love Canal.
But they never end. Invisible contaminants remain a part of the sur-

roundings, absorbed into the grain of the landscape, the tissues of the body, and, worst of all, the genetic material of the survivors. An all clear is never sounded. The book of accounts is never closed.

. . .

For many people, to be exposed to radiation or other forms of toxicity is to be contaminated in some deep and lasting way, to feel dirtied, tainted, corrupted. "It will always be there, the contamination," said one woman of sixty, speaking of both herself and the world around her. A neighbor of hers, a man of forty-eight, added: "I don't feel that the stuff is going to leave. It's still here with us. It's in our bodies, in our genes, and later on we're going to pay for it."

. . .

Radiation and most other toxic substances are without body. One cannot taste them, touch them, smell them, or see them, and for that reason they seem especially ghostlike and terrifying. Moreover, they invert the process by which disasters normally do harm. They do not charge in from outside and batter like a gust of wind or a wall of water. They slink in without warning, do no immediate damage so far as one can tell, and then begin their deadly work from within—the very embodiment of stealth and treachery.

The widely observed prohibition against chemical warfare might be instructive here. Chemical weapons clearly have a special place on the human list of horrors, but why that should be so is not at all obvious. In World War I, for example, shrapnel proved a good deal more lethal than gas, but no one seems to have suggested that it be outlawed on that account, presumably because it does such a straightforward job of ripping through flesh and tearing bodies apart. So the moral case must lie in the way the two work rather than in the amount of damage they do. "Gas is a perfidious, impalpable, and cruel abomination," said an Allied report shortly after the war[11] ("that hellish poison" Winston Churchill called it), and that puts the case plainly enough. It is furtive, invisible, unnatural. In most of its forms it moves for the interior, turning the process of assault inside out and in that way violating the integrity of the body. A sociologist, again, may have no warrant to suggest that this aversion stems from something elemental in the human spirit, but in this instance, at least, we have historical records to draw on, for poison has always represented the epitome of evil and treachery in the way we tell the story of our past.

. . . Toxic poisons provoke a special dread because they contaminate, because they are stealthy and deceive the body's alarm systems, and because they can become absorbed into the very tissues of the body and crouch there for years, even generations, before doing their deadly work. A number of people from Three Mile Island . . . note that it is as if they had "a time bomb ticking" within them.

All of the above may suggest that people will not so easily become "unscared" of radiation and other forms of toxicity with the passing of time. And if that is what fate has in store for us, a new set of questions rises quickly to the surface: What happens to people who experience this kind of dread over long stretches of time? What will be the consequence if that dread finds a more and more permanent place in the human imagination?

People exposed to disasters are very apt to develop a sense of being out of control, of being caught up in forces that capture them and take them over. Feelings of helplessness and vulnerability are so common in moments of crisis, I noted earlier, that they are recognized as one of the identifying psychological symptoms of "trauma" and a prominent feature of what is often called the disaster syndrome. Two . . . witnesses from Three Mile Island:

> Fear, that's what it is. Afraid. You're sitting at the edge of your seat. It's like we're in their hands. It's like we're being manipulated by a couple of stacks.

> I don't know how to explain it. I just feel insecure. I just feel scared, afraid. It's just like being in an airplane and you're afraid because you don't know [anything about] the pilot.

Survivors of severe disasters, that is to say, experience not just a sense of vulnerability but a feeling of having lost a certain immunity to misfortune, a feeling, even, that something terrible is almost *bound* to happen. They come to feel . . . that the blow visiting them "was not just a freak act of nature or a vicious act of men but a sample of what the universe has in store for them."[12] One of the crucial jobs of culture, let's say, is to help people camouflage the actual risks of the world around them—to help them edit reality in such a way that it seems manageable, to help them edit it in such a way that the perils pressing in on all sides are screened out of their line of vision as they go about their daily rounds. . . .

This kind of emotional insulation is stripped away, at least for the moment, in most severe disasters, but with a special sharpness in events like the ones we have been considering here exactly because one can never assume that they are over. What must it be like, having just discovered through bitter experience that reality is a thing of unrelenting danger, to have to look those dangers straight in the eye without blinders or filters? Let's return to our witnesses from Three Mile Island:

> Scary. Like you pull in the driveway, and you think "when I walk into the house will there be some kind of radiation lingering?" It came into your house and it's going to stay there. You think "is the food in the refrigerator safe to eat?" So you still have that insecure feeling of wondering what is going to happen at TMI. Are they telling us everything? . . . You always have that insecure feeling. I'll always have it.

> And the radio, to this day, plays all the time in my house. I have to know if anything happens. . . . Something like that just hanging over us constantly. I hate it. I just hate it.

People stripped of the ability to screen out signs of peril are not just unusually vigilant and unusually anxious. They evaluate the data of everyday life differently, read the signs differently, see patterns that the rest of us are for the most part spared.

> My mind is like a little computer. It's always ticking. . . . I figure it even ticks when I'm asleep. I listen more to what people say to me. It's hard to trust. Only the ones close to you

it seems you can trust. I'm not being paranoid or nothing. It's not like that. It's just that these last couple of years . . . I see more now, I listen to more of what people say. I read between the lines more.

Once victims reach that level of awareness, evidence that the world is a place of constant peril appears everywhere. It is a rare morning newspaper or evening broadcast that does not contain news of acid rain, polluted beaches, tank car derailments, newly discovered toxic waste dumps, or malfunctions at nuclear power plants (all of which are stories in the news as I write these pages). The following stories, for example, were among scores clipped from the two newspapers I read within a few days: "Plutonium Hazard Found at Nuclear Power Plant," "Polluted Lake Belowground Worries EPA," "Entire Town in Ohio Evacuated in Gas Leak," "Dioxin Found in Milk from Paper Cartons," "Oil Spill Shuts, 30-Mile Stretch of Hudson River," "Pollution Poses Growing Threat to Everglades," "Mill Town Agonizes over High Dioxin Readings," and "Nuclear Reactor in Spain Catches Fire." If these are the kinds of data your mind is sensitive to, the kinds of data your eye, made sharp and canny by events of the recent past, is good at taking in, the gloomiest of forecasts can seem amply supported.

. . .

The most important point to be made here is that when the dread is lasting and pronounced, the spectacle of a failed technology can become the spectacle of a failed environment as well. This is an outlook born of the sense that poisons are now lodged in the tissues of the body, that the surrounding countryside is contaminated as well, that the whole natural envelope in which people live out their lives has become defiled and unreliable. "Dead ground," said one person from Three Mile Island, speaking of the land he was standing on. But he did not mean that it was inert and lifeless like a moonscape. It was, for him, alive with dangers, a terrain in which fresh air and sunshine and all the other benevolences of creation are to be feared as sources of toxic infection.

. . .

Indeed, everything out there can seem unreliable and fearsome. The vegetables in one's own garden can no longer be depended on ("I went down there and I cut [the asparagus] off and threw it into the weeds. . . . The stuff around here that was growing in the ground was not fit to eat because it was radiated"). The river can no longer be depended on ("The water's polluted and doesn't even freeze up anymore"). The ground itself can no longer be relied on ("We had a very nice yard. Now nothing grows. The land is bad"). People feel that something noxious is closing in on them, drifting down from above, creeping up from underneath, edging in sideways, fouling the very air and insinuating itself in all the objects and spaces that make up their surroundings.

"Well, why don't you move to a safer location?" they are asked. But that is to misunderstand, for there *is* no safer location. The point is not that a particular region is now spoiled but that the whole world has been revealed as a place of danger and numbing uncertainty: "The whole country. There's no place in this country that you could go to that isn't slopped up. . . . There isn't a safe place that you could go to that the drinking water isn't bad. The food you get is all poisoned. There's radiation. . . . It isn't like it was when we were kids."

It is important to note . . . that these voices express a fear and a view of the world shared by a portion of the people of Three Mile Island—and, for that matter, of the people living in other emergency sites where researchers have posted themselves to listen. I am not trying to suggest that all survivors of a toxic emergency see things as they do. The portion that does, however, is large by any measure. And the fact that waves of people share a common dread not only in such well-known places as Love Canal and Three Mile Island, Chernobyl and Bhopal but, also in lesser-known disaster sites like Centralia (Pennsylvania), Legler (New Jersey), Times Beach (Missouri), and Woburn (Massachusetts) . . . should tell us that something important may be happening here, for the apprehension that appears to be so widely spread throughout the population can easily erupt into the feelings expressed above.[13]

. . .

*Э*ndnotes

[1]Flynn, C. B. (1981) Three Mile Island Telephone Survey: Preliminary Report on Procedures and Findings (NUREG/CR-1093, U.S. Nuclear Regulatory Commission). Zeigler, D. J., Brunn, S. D. & Johnson, J. H. Jr., Evacuation from a nuclear technological disaster. *Geographical Review, 71,*1–16.

[2]Zeigler, Brunn, & Johnson, *op. cit.*

[3]Perrow, C. (1984). *Normal accidents* New York: Basic. 1984.

[4]This would give us a four-cell table of roughly the following sort

The first cell would contain technological mishaps like explosions and collisions; the second would contain the usual gatherings of floods,

	Technological	Natural
Non-Toxic	a	b
Toxic	c	d

earthquakes, storms, and so on; the third would contain events like the ones described in this essay—Chernobyl and Bhopal, Love Canal and Three Mile Island, Grassy Narrows and East Swallow—and the fourth would contain natural forms of toxic poisoning like radon. We will need a more complex diagram eventually—some kind of scatter plot, probably—since some events need to be represented as closer to the lines separating technological from natural and toxic from nontoxic than others. But that is another problem for another time.

[5]See Slovic, P., Lichtenstein, S. & Fischoff, B. (1979). Images of disaster: Perception and acceptance of risks from nuclear power. In G. Goodman and W. Rowe (Eds.), *Energy risk management.* New York: Academic. Slovic, F., & Lichtenstein (1980). Rating the risks. *Environment, 21,* 14–38. Slovic, F., & Lichtenstein (1980). Facts and fears: understanding perceived risk. In R. C. Schwing & W. A. Albers, Jr. (1980). *Societal Risk Assessment.* New York: Plenum. Slovic & Fischoff. (1983). How safe is safe enough? Determinants of perceived and acceptable risk. In

C. A. Walker, L. C. Gould, & E. J. Woodhouse (Eds.), New Haven: Yale University Press. And so on . . .

[6]Social Data Analysts. (1982). Attitudes toward evacuation: Reactions of Long Island residents to a possible accident at the Shoreham nuclear power station. Report prepared for Suffolk County New York. Johnson, J. H., Jr., & Zeigler, D. J. (1982, November). Further analysis and interpretation of the Shoreham Evacuation Survey. (Vol. III). Suffolk County Radiological Emergency Response Plan. Zeigler, D. J., Johnson, J. H., Jr., & Brunn, S. D. (1983). *Technological hazards* Washington, DC: Association of American Geographers.

[7]Kunreuther, H., DesVouges, W. H., & Slovic, P. (1988, October). Nevada's predicament: Public perceptions of risk from the proposed nuclear waste repository. *Environment, 30,* 17–20, 30–33.

[8]Weinberg, A. M. (1976). The maturity and future of nuclear energy. *American Scientist, 64,* 16–21.

[9]See Brown, P., & Mikkelson, E. J. (1990). *No safe place: Toxic waste, leukemia, and community action.* Berkeley: University of California Press. Edelstein, M. (1988). *Contaminated communities: The social and psychological impacts of residential toxic exposure.* Boulder, CO: Westview Press. Houts, P. (1989). *The Three Mile Island crisis.* University Park, PA: Pennsylvania State University Press. Kroll-Smith, J. S., & Couch, S. R. (1990). *The real disaster is above ground.* Lexington, KY: University . of Kentucky Press. Levine, A. G. (1982). *Love canal: Science, politics and people.* Lexington, MA: Lexington Books. Reko, H. K. (1984). *Not an act of God: Story of Times Beach.* St. Louis, MO: Ecumenical Dioxin Response Task. Shkilnyk, A. M. (1985). *A poison stronger than love: The destruction of an Ojibway community.* New Haven: Yale University Press.

[10]Aristotle, (1932). *The Poetics.* (W. H. Fyve Trans.). Cambridge, MA: Harvard University Press, pp. 29–31.

[11]Brown, F. J. (1968). *Chemical warfare: A study in restraints.* Princeton: University Press, p. 18.

[12]Erikson, K. (1976). *Everything in its path.* New York: Simon & Schuster, p. 236.

[13]For Love Canal, see Levine, note 9; for Three Mile Island, Houts; for Centralia, Kroll-Smith and Couch; for East Swallow, Erikson; for Grassy

Narrows, Shkilnyk; for Legler, Edelstein; for Times Beach, Reko; for Woburn, Brown and Mikkelson.

❂ ❂ ❂

Questions

1. What is the "new species of trouble" that the author addesses? What differentiates these new troubles from the old species of troubles?

2. Why did the accident at Three Mile Island evoke such widespread evacuation?

3. What are technological disasters? How do they differ from natural disasters

4. What are normal accidents? Give an example.

5. If you had been living near Three Mile Island at the time of the accident, how would you have responded? Explain.

The Code of the Streets

ELIJAH ANDERSON

As you might guess, urban enclaves have their own culture. Unfortunately, it is often characterized by norms of violence and aggression. In this selection, Elijah Anderson gives us a glimpse at the "code of the streets" that governs social relations among the urban poor. He also details the difficult balancing act that "decent" folks must perform to strive for upward mobility while maintaining respect in their own communities.

Of all the problems besetting the poor inner-city black community, none is more pressing than that of interpersonal violence and aggression. It wreaks havoc daily with the lives of community residents and increasingly spills over into downtown and residential middle-class areas. Muggings, burglaries, carjackings, and drug-related shootings, all of which may leave their victims or innocent bystanders dead, are now common enough to concern all urban and many suburban residents. The inclination to violence springs from the circumstances of life among the ghetto-poor—the lack of jobs that pay a living wage, the stigma of race, the fallout from rampant drug use and drug trafficking, and the resulting alienation and lack of hope for the future.

Simply living in such an environment places young people at special risk falling victim to aggressive behavior. Although there are often forces in the community which can counteract the negative influences, by far the most powerful being a strong, loving, "decent" (as inner-city residents put it) family committed to middle-class values, the despair is pervasive enough to have spawned an oppositional culture, that of "the streets," whose norms are often consciously opposed to those of mainstream society. These two orientations—decent and street—socially organize the community, and their coexistence has important consequences for residents, particularly children growing up in the inner city. Above all, this environment means that even youngsters whose home lives reflect mainstream values—and the majority of homes in the community do—must be able to handle themselves in a street-oriented environment.

"The Code of the Streets," by Elijah Anderson, reprinted from *The Atlantic Monthly*, Vol. 273, No. 5, May 1994. Copyright © 1994 by Elijah Anderson.

This is because the street culture has evolved what may be called a code of the streets, which amounts to a set of informal rules governing interpersonal public behavior, including violence. The rules prescribe both a proper comportment and a proper way to respond if challenged. They regulate the use of violence and so allow those who are inclined to aggression to precipitate violent encounters in an approved way. The rules have been established and are enforced mainly by the street-oriented, but on the streets the distinction between street and decent is often irrelevant; everybody knows that if the rules are violated, there are penalties. Knowledge of the code is thus largely defensive; it is literally necessary for operating in public. Therefore, even though families with a decency orientation are usually opposed to the values of the code, they often reluctantly encourage their children's familiarity with it to enable them to negotiate the inner-city environment.

At the heart of the code is the issue of respect—loosely defined as being treated "right," or granted the deference one deserves. However, in the troublesome public environment of the inner city, as people increasingly feel buffeted by forces beyond their control, what one deserves in the way of respect becomes more and more problematic and uncertain. This in turn further opens the issue of respect to sometimes intense interpersonal negotiation. In the street culture, especially among young people, respect is viewed as almost an external entity that is hard-won but easily lost, and so must constantly be guarded. The rules of the code in fact provide a framework for negotiating respect. The person whose very appearance—including his clothing, demeanor, and way of moving—deters transgressions feels that he possesses, and may be considered by others to possess, a measure of respect. With the right amount of respect, for instance, he can avoid "being bothered" in public. If he is bothered, not only may he be in physical danger but he has been disgraced or "dissed" (disrespected). Many of the forms that dissing can take might seem petty to middle-class people (maintaining eye contact for too long, for example), but to those invested in the street code, these actions become serious indications of the other person's intentions. Consequently, such people become very sensitive to advances and slights, which could well serve as warnings of imminent physical confrontation.

This hard reality can be traced to the profound sense of alienation from mainstream society and its institutions felt by many poor inner-city black people, particularly the young. The code of the streets is actually a cultural adaptation to a profound lack of faith in the police and the judicial system. The police are most often seen as representing the dominant white society and not caring to protect inner-city residents. When called, they may not respond, which is one reason many residents feel they must be prepared to take extraordinary measures to defend themselves and their loved ones against those who are inclined to aggression. Lack of police accountability has in fact been incorporated into the status system: the person who is believed capable of "taking care of himself" is accorded a certain deference, which translates into a sense of physical and psychological control. Thus the street code emerges where the influence of the police ends and personal responsibility for one's safety is felt to begin. Exacerbated by the proliferation of drugs and easy access to guns, this volatile situation results in the ability of the street-oriented minority (or those who effectively "go for bad") to dominate the public spaces.

⊛ Decent and Street Families

Although almost everyone in poor inner-city neighborhoods is struggling financially and therefore feels a certain distance from the rest of America, the decent and the street family in a real sense represent two poles of value orientation, two contrasting conceptual categories. The labels "decent" and "street," which the residents themselves use, amount to evaluative judgments that confer status on local residents. The labeling is often the result of a social contest among the individuals and families of the neighborhood. Individuals of the two orientations often coexist in the same extended family. Decent residents judge themselves to be so while judging others to be of the street, and street individuals often present themselves as decent, drawing distinctions between themselves and other people. In addition, there is quite a bit of circumstantial behavior—that is, one person may at different times exhibit both decent and street orientations, depending on the circumstances. Although these designations result from so much social jockeying, there do exist concrete features that define each conceptual category.

Generally, so-called decent families tend to accept mainstream values more fully and attempt to instill them in their children. Whether married couples with children or single-parent (usually female) households, they are generally "working poor" and so tend to be better off financially than their street-oriented neighbors. They value hard work and self-reliance and are willing to sacrifice for their children. Because they have a certain amount of faith in mainstream society, they harbor hopes for a better future for their children, if not for themselves. Many of them go to church and take a strong interest in their children's schooling. Rather than dwelling on the real hardships and inequities facing them, many such decent people, particularly the increasing number of grandmothers raising grandchildren, see their difficult situation as a test from God and derive great support from their faith and from the church community.

Extremely aware of the problematic and often dangerous environment in which they reside, decent parents tend to be strict in their child-rearing practices, encouraging children to respect authority and walk a straight moral line. They have an almost obsessive concern about trouble of any kind and remind their children to be on the lookout for people and situations that might lead to it. At the same time, they are themselves polite and considerate of others, and teach their children to be the same way. At home, at work, and in church, they strive hard to maintain a positive mental attitude and a spirit of cooperation.

So-called street parents, in contrast, often show a lack of consideration for other people and have a rather superficial sense of family and community. Though they may love their children, many of them are unable to cope with the physical and emotional demands of parenthood, and find it difficult to reconcile their needs with those of their children. These families, who are more fully invested in the code of the streets than the decent people are, may aggressively socialize their children into it in a normative way. They believe in the code and judge themselves and others according to its values.

In fact the overwhelming majority of families in the inner-city community try to approximate the decent-family model, but there are many others who clearly represent the worst fears of the decent family. Not only are their financial resources extremely limited, but what little they have may easily be misused. The lives of the street-oriented are often marked by disorganization. In the most desperate circumstances people frequently have a limited understanding of priorities and consequences, and so frustrations mount over bills, food, and, at times, drink, cigarettes, and drugs. Some tend toward self-destructive behavior; many street-oriented women are crack-addicted ("on the pipe"), alcoholic, or involved in complicated relationships with men who abuse them. In addition, the seeming intractability of their situation, caused in large part by the lack of well-paying jobs and the persistence of racial discrimination, has engendered deep-seated bitterness and anger in many of the most desperate and poorest blacks, especially young people. The need both to exercise a measure of control and to lash out at somebody is often reflected in the adults' relations with their children. At the least, the frustrations of persistent poverty shorten the fuse in such people—contributing to a lack of patience with anyone, child or adult, who irritates them.

In these circumstances a woman—or a man, although men are less consistently present in children's lives—can be quite aggressive with children, yelling at and striking them for the least little infraction of the rules she has set down. Often little if any serious explanation follows the verbal and physical punishment. This response teaches children a particular lesson. They learn that to solve any kind of interpersonal problem one must quickly resort to hitting or other violent behavior. Actual peace and quiet, and also the appearance of calm, respectful children conveyed to her neighbors and friends, are often what the young mother most desires, but at times she will be very aggressive in trying to get them. Thus she may be quick to beat her children, especially if they defy her law, not because she hates them but because this is the way she knows to control them. In fact, many street-oriented women love their children dearly. Many mothers in the community subscribe to the notion that there is a "devil in the boy" that must be beaten out of him or that socially "fast girls need to be whupped." Thus much of what borders on child abuse in the view of social authorities is acceptable parental punishment in the view of these mothers.

Many street-oriented women are sporadic mothers whose children learn to fend for themselves when necessary, foraging for food and money any way they can get it. The children are sometimes employed by drug dealers or become addicted themselves. These children of the street, growing up with little supervision, are said to "come up hard." They often learn to fight at an early age, sometimes using short-tempered adults around them as role models. The street-oriented home may be fraught with anger, verbal disputes, physical aggression, and even mayhem. The children observe these goings-on, learning the lesson that might makes right. They quickly learn to hit those who cross them, and the dog-eat-dog mentality prevails. In order to survive, to protect oneself, it is necessary to marshal inner resources and be ready to deal with adversity in a hands-on way. In these circumstances physical prowess takes on great significance.

In some of the most desperate cases, a street-oriented mother may simply leave her young children alone and unattended while she goes out. The most irresponsible women can be found at local bars and crack houses, getting high and socializing with other adults. Sometimes a troubled woman will leave very young children alone for days at a time. Reports of crack addicts abandoning their children have become common in drug-infested inner-city communities. Neighbors or relatives discover the abandoned children, often hungry and distraught over the absence of their mother. After repeated absences, a friend or relative, particularly a grandmother, will often step in to care for the young children, sometimes petitioning the authorities to send her, as guardian of the children, the mother's welfare check, if the mother gets one. By this time, however, the children may well have learned the first lesson of the streets; survival itself, let alone respect, cannot be taken for granted; you have to fight for your place in the world.

❦ Campaigning for Respect

. . . When decent and street kids come together, a kind of social shuffle occurs in which children have a chance to go either way. Tension builds as a child comes to realize that he must choose an orientation. The kind of home he comes from influences but does not determine the way he will ultimately turn out—although it is unlikely that a child from a thoroughly street-oriented family will easily absorb decent values on the streets. Youths who emerge from street-oriented families but develop a decency orientation almost always learn those values in another setting—in school, in a youth group, in church. Often it is the result of their involvement with a caring "old head" (adult role model).

In the street, through their play, children pour their individual life experiences into a common knowledge pool, affirming, confirming, and elaborating on what they have observed in the home and matching their skills against those of others. And they learn to fight. Even small children test one another, pushing and shoving, and are ready to hit other children over circumstances not to their liking. In turn, they are readily hit by other children, and the child who is toughest prevails. Thus the violent resolution of disputes, the hitting and cursing, gains social reinforcement. The child in effect is initiated into a system that is really a way of campaigning for respect.

In addition, younger children witness the disputes of older children, which are often resolved through cursing and abusive talk, if not aggression or outright violence. They see that one child succumbs to the greater physical and mental abilities of the other. They are also alert and attentive witnesses to the verbal and physical fights of adults, after which they compare notes and share their interpretations of the event. In almost every case the victor is the person who physically won the altercation, and this person often enjoys the esteem and respect of onlookers. These experiences reinforce the lessons the children have learned at home: might makes right, and toughness is a virtue, while humility is not. In effect they learn the social meaning of fighting. When it is left virtually unchallenged, this understanding becomes an ever more important part of the child's working conception of the world. Over time the code of the streets becomes refined.

Those street-oriented adults with whom children come in contact—including mothers, fathers, brothers, sisters, boyfriends, cousins, neighbors, and friends—help them along in forming this understanding by verbalizing the messages they are getting through experience: "Watch your back." "Protect yourself." "Don't punk out." "If somebody messes with you, you got to pay them back." "If someone disses you, you got to straighten them out." Many parents actually impose sanctions if a child is not sufficiently aggressive. For example, if a child loses a fight and comes home upset, the parent might respond, "Don't you come in here crying that somebody beat you up; you better get back out there and whup his ass. I didn't raise no punks! Get back out there and whup his ass. If you don't whup his ass, I'll whup your ass when you come home." Thus the child obtains reinforcement for being tough and showing nerve. . . .

❂ Self-Image Based on "Juice"

By the time they are teenagers, most youths have either internalized the code of the streets or at least learned the need to comport themselves in accordance with its rules, which chiefly have to do with interpersonal communication. The code revolves around the presentation of self. Its basic requirement is the display of a certain predisposition to violence. Accordingly, one's bearing must send the unmistakable if sometimes subtle message to "the next person" in public that one is capable of violence and mayhem when the situation requires it, that one can take care of oneself. The nature of this communication is largely determined by the demands of the circumstances but can include facial expressions, gait, and verbal expressions—all of which are geared mainly to deterring aggression. Physical appearance, including clothes, jewelry, and grooming, also plays an important part in how a person is viewed; to be respected, it is important to have the right look.

Even so, there are no guarantees against challenges, because there are always people around looking for a fight to increase their share of respect—or "juice," as it is sometimes called on the street. Moreover, if a person is assaulted, it is important, not only in the eyes of his opponent but also in the eyes of his "running buddies," for him to avenge himself. Otherwise he risks being "tried" (challenged) or "moved on" by any number of others. To maintain his honor he must show he is not someone to be "messed with" or "dissed." In general, the person must "keep himself straight" by managing his position of respect among others; this involves in part his self-image, which is shaped by what he thinks others are thinking of him in relation to his peers.

Objects play an important and complicated role in establishing self-image. Jackets, sneakers, gold jewelry, reflect not just a person's taste, which tends to be tightly regulated among adolescents of all social classes, but also a willingness to possess things that may require defending. A boy wearing a fashionable, expensive jacket, for example, is vulnerable to attack by another who covets the jacket and either cannot afford to buy one or wants the added satisfaction of depriving someone else of his. However, if the boy forgoes the desirable jacket and wears one that isn't "hip," he runs the risk of being teased and possibly even assaulted as an unworthy person. To be allowed to hang with certain prestigious crowds, a boy must wear a different set of expensive clothes—sneakers and athletic suit—every day. Not to be able to do so might make him appear socially deficient. The youth comes to covet such items—especially when he sees easy prey wearing them.

In acquiring valued things, therefore, a person shores up his identity—but since it is an identity based on having things, it is highly precarious. This very precariousness gives a heightened sense of urgency to staying even with peers, with whom the person is actually competing. Young men and women who are able to command respect through their presentation of self—by allowing their possessions and their body language to speak for them—may not have to campaign for regard but may, rather, gain it by the force of their manner. Those who are unable to command respect in this way must actively campaign for it—and are thus particularly alive to slights.

One way of campaigning for status is by taking the possessions of others. In this context, seemingly ordinary objects can become trophies imbued with symbolic value that far exceeds their monetary worth. Possession of the trophy can symbolize the ability to violate somebody—to "get in his face," to take something of value from him, to "dis" him, and thus to enhance one's own worth by stealing someone else's. The trophy does not have to be something material. It can be another person's sense of honor, snatched away with a derogatory remark. It can be the outcome of a fight. It can be the imposition of a certain standard, such as a girl's getting herself recognized as the most beautiful. Material things, however, fit easily into the pattern. Sneakers, a pistol, even somebody else's girlfriend, can become a trophy. When a person can take something from another and then flaunt it, he gains a certain regard by being the owner, or the controller, of that thing. But this display of ownership can then provoke other people to challenge him. This game of who controls what is thus constantly being played out on inner-city streets, and the trophy—extrinsic or intrinsic, tangible or intangible—identifies the current winner.

An important aspect of this often violent give-and-take is its zero-sum quality. That is, the extent to which one person can raise himself up depends on his ability to put another person down. This underscores the alienation that permeates the inner-city ghetto community. There is a generalized sense that very little respect is to be had, and therefore everyone competes to get what affirmation he can of the little that is available. The craving for respect that results gives people thin skins. Shows of deference by others can be highly soothing, contributing to a sense of security, comfort, self-confidence, and self-respect. Transgressions by others which go unanswered diminish these feelings and are believed to encourage further transgressions. Hence one must be ever vigilant against the transgressions of others or even appearing as if transgressions will be tolerated. Among young people, whose sense of self-esteem is particularly vulnerable, there is an especially heightened concern with being disrespected. Many inner-city young men in particular crave respect to such a degree that they will risk their lives to attain and maintain it.

The issue of respect is thus closely tied to whether a person has an inclination to be violent, even as a victim. In the wider society people may not feel required to retaliate physically after an attack, even though they are aware that they have been degraded or taken advantage of. They may feel a great need to defend themselves during an attack, or to behave in such a way as to deter aggression (middle-class people certainly can and do become victims of street-oriented youths), but they are much more likely than street-oriented people to feel that they can walk away from a possible altercation with their self-esteem intact. Some people may even have the strength of character to flee, without any thought that their self-respect or esteem will be diminished.

In impoverished inner-city black communities, however, particularly among young males and perhaps increasingly among females, such flight would be extremely difficult. To run away would likely leave one's self-esteem in tatters. Hence people often feel constrained not only to stand up and at least attempt to resist during an assault but also to "pay back"—to seek revenge—after a successful assault on their person. This may include going to get a weapon or even getting relatives involved. Their very identity and self-respect, their honor, is often intricately tied up with the way they perform on the streets during and after such encounters. This outlook reflects the circumscribed opportunities of the inner-city poor. Generally people outside the ghetto have other ways of gaining status and regard, and thus do not feel so dependent on such physical displays.

❧ By Trial of Manhood

On the street, among males these concerns about things and identity have come to be expressed in the concept of "manhood." Manhood in the inner city means taking the prerogatives of men with respect to strangers, other men, and women—being distinguished as a man. It implies physicality and a certain ruthlessness. Regard and respect are associated with this concept in large part because of its practical application: if others have little or no regard for a person's manhood, his very life and those of his loved ones could be in jeopardy. But there is a chicken-and-egg aspect to this situation: one's physical safety is more likely to be jeopardized in public because manhood is associated with respect. In other words, an existential link has been created between the idea of manhood and one's self-esteem, so that it has become hard to say which is primary. For many inner-city youths, manhood and respect are flip sides of the same coin; physical and psychological well-being are inseparable, and both require a sense of control, of being in charge.

The operating assumption is that a man, especially a real man, knows what other men know—the code of the streets. And if one is not a real man, one is somehow diminished as a person, and there are certain valued things one simply does not deserve. There is thus believed to be a certain justice to the code, since it is considered that everyone has the opportunity to know it. Implicit in this is that everybody is held responsible for being familiar with the code. If the victim of a mugging, for example, does not know the code and so responds "wrong," the perpetrator may feel justified even in killing him and may feel no remorse. He may think, "Too bad, but it's his fault. He should have known better." . . .

Central to the issue of manhood is the widespread belief that one of the most effective ways of gaining respect is to manifest "nerve." Nerve is shown when one takes another person's possessions (the more valuable the better), "messes with" someone's woman, throws the first punch, "gets in someone's face," or pulls a trigger. Its proper display helps on the spot to check others who would violate one's person and also helps to build a reputation that works to prevent future challenges. But since such a show of nerve is a forceful expression of disrespect toward the person on the receiving end, the victim may be greatly offended and seek to retaliate with equal or greater force. A display of nerve, therefore, can easily provoke a life-threatening response, and the background knowledge of that possibility has often been incorporated into the concept of nerve. . . .

❧ Girls and Boys

Increasingly, teenage girls are mimicking the boys and trying to have their own version of "manhood." Their goal is the same—to get respect, to be recognized as capable of setting or maintaining a certain standard. They try to achieve this end in the ways that have been established by the boys, including posturing, abusive language, and the use of violence to resolve disputes, but the issues for the girls are different. Although conflicts over turf and status exist among the girls, the majority of disputes seem rooted in assessments of beauty (which girl in a group is "the cutest"), competition over boyfriends, and attempts to regulate other people's knowledge of and opinions about a girl's behavior or that of someone close to her, especially her mother.

A major cause of conflicts among girls is "he say, she say." This practice begins in the early school years and continues through high school. It occurs when "people," particularly girls, talk about others, thus putting their "business in the streets." Usually one girl will say something negative about another in the group, most often behind the person's back. The remark will then get back to the person talked about. She may retaliate or her friends may feel required to "take up for" her. In essence this is a form of group gossiping in which individuals are negatively assessed and evaluated. As with much gossip, the things said may or may not be true, but the point is that such imputations can cast aspersions on a person's good name. The accused is required to defend herself against the slander, which can result in arguments and fights, often over little of real substance. Here again is the problem of low self-esteem, which encourages youngsters to be highly sensitive to slights and to be vulnerable to feeling easily "dissed." To avenge the dissing, a fight is usually necessary.

Because boys are believed to control violence, girls tend to defer to them in situations of conflict. Often if a girl is attacked or feels slighted, she will get a brother, uncle, or cousin to do her fighting for her. Increasingly, however, girls are doing their own fighting and are even asking their male relatives to teach them how to fight. Some girls form groups that attack other girls or take things from them. A hard-core segment of inner-city girls inclined toward violence seems to be developing. As one thirteen-year-old girl in a detention center for youths who have committed violent acts told me, "To get people to leave you alone, you gotta fight. Talking don't always get you out of stuff." One major difference between girls and boys: girls rarely use guns. Their fights are therefore not life-or-death struggles. Girls are not often willing to put their lives on the line for "manhood." The ultimate form of respect on the male-dominated inner-city street is thus reserved for men.

❧ "Going for Bad"

In the most fearsome youths such a cavalier attitude toward death grows out of a very limited view of life. Many are uncertain about how long they are going to live and believe they could die violently at any time. They accept this fate; they live on the edge. Their manner conveys the message that nothing intimidates them; whatever turn the encounter takes, they maintain their attack—rather like a pit bull, whose spirit many such boys admire. The demonstration of such tenacity "shows heart" and earns their respect.

This fearlessness has implications for law enforcement. Many street-oriented boys are much more concerned about the threat of "justice" at the hands of a peer than at the hands of the police. Moreover, many feel not only that they have little to lose by going to prison but that they have something to gain. The toughening-up one experiences in prison can actually enhance one's reputation on the streets. Hence the system loses influence over the hard core who are without jobs, with little perceptible stake in the system. If mainstream society has done nothing for them, they counter by making sure it can do nothing to them.

At the same time, however, a competing view maintains that true nerve consists in backing down, walking away from a fight, and going on with one's business. One fights only in self-defense. This view emerges from the decent philosophy that life is precious, and it is an important part of the socialization process common in decent homes. It discourages violence as the primary means of resolving disputes and encourages youngsters to accept nonviolence and talk as confrontational strategies. . . .

Although the nonviolent orientation rarely overcomes the impulse to strike back in an encounter, it does introduce a certain confusion and so can prompt a measure of soul-searching, or even profound ambivalence. Did the person back down with his respect intact or did he back down only to be judged a "punk"—a person lacking manhood? Should he or she have acted? Should he or she have hit the other person in the mouth? These questions best many young men and women during public confrontations. What is the "right" thing to do? In the quest for honor, respect, and local status—which few young people are uninterested in—common sense most often prevails, which leads many to opt for the tough approach, enacting their own particular versions of the display of nerve. The presentation of oneself as rough and tough is very often quite acceptable until one is tested. And then that presentation may help the person pass the test, because it will cause fewer questions to be asked about what he did and why. It is hard for a person to explain why he lost the fight or why he backed down. Hence many will strive to appear to "go for bad," while hoping they will never be tested. But when they are tested, the outcome of the situation may quickly be out of their hands, as they become wrapped up in the circumstances of the moment.

❧ An Oppositional Culture

The attitudes of the wider society are deeply implicated in the code of the streets. Most people in inner-city communities are not totally invested in the code, but the significant minority of hard-core street youths who are have to maintain the code in order to establish reputations, because they have—or feel they have—few other ways to assert themselves. For these young people the standards of the street code are the only game in town. The extent to which some children—particularly those who through upbringing have become most alienated and those lacking in strong and conventional social support—experience, feel, and internalize racist rejection and contempt from mainstream society may strongly encourage them to express contempt for the more conventional society in turn. In dealing with this contempt and rejection, some youngsters will consciously invest themselves and their considerable mental resources in what amounts to an oppositional culture to preserve themselves and their self-respect. Once they do, any respect they might be able to garner in the wider system pales in comparison with the respect available in the local system; thus they often lose interest in even attempting to negotiate the mainstream system.

At the same time, many less alienated young blacks have assumed a street-oriented demeanor as a way of expressing their blackness while really embracing a much more moderate way of life; they, too, want a nonviolent setting in which to live and raise a family. These decent people are trying hard to be part of the mainstream culture, but the racism, real and perceived, that they encounter helps to legitimate the oppositional culture. And so on occasion they adopt street behavior. In fact, depending on the demands of the situation, many people in the community slip back and forth between decent and street behavior.

A vicious cycle has thus been formed. The hopelessness and alienation many young inner-city black men and women feel, largely as a result of endemic joblessness and persistent racism, fuels the violence they engage in.

This violence serves to confirm the negative feelings many whites and some middle-class blacks harbor toward the ghetto poor, further legitimating the oppositional culture and the code of the streets in the eyes of many poor young blacks. Unless this cycle is broken, attitudes on both sides will become increasingly entrenched, and the violence, which claims victims black and white, poor and affluent, will only escalate.

۞ ۞ ۞

Questions

1. What is the difference between "decent" and "street" folks? Do they share any similarities? If so, what are they?

2. What is the code of the streets? What caused the emergence of this code? What kind of changes would have to occur to change the code of the streets?

3. Respect is a crucial element in urban areas. How do youths try to get and maintain respect? How important are commodities or "things" in the effort to gain respect?

4. Compare and contrast the normative definitions governing respect and behavior for urban men and women.

5. How do youth from "decent families" balance the oppositional cultural demands made on them by their peers (through street culture) and their family (through "decent" culture)? What are some social, economic, and psychological costs of this balancing act?

Names, Logos, Mascots, and Flags: The Contradictory Uses of Sport Symbols

STANLEY EITZEN

Symbols are powerful forms of communication, but they often have different meanings from different groups of people. An extended thumb and pinkie represents "hang 10" in California, "hook 'em horns" in Texas, and "call me" when held up to one's ear in most other locales.

In this selection, Stanley Eitzen examines the prevalence and potentially divisive effects of athletic teams using symbols, logos, mascots, and flags. Eitzen discusses the powerful effect that symbols have when applied to athletic teams—especially as they relate to the confederate south, Native Americans and their culture, and women. These symbols can unite members of a group by building a sense of shared identity, but they can also separate groups and reinforce status differences.

The two teams that played in the 1995 World Series were the Atlanta Braves and the Cleveland Indians. Inside the stadium, the fans of the Braves did the "tomahawk chop" and enthusiastically shouted "Indian" chants. Similarly, the fans of the Indians united behind their symbol, Chief Wahoo, waved foam tomahawks, and wore war paint and other pseudo–Native American symbols. Outside the stadium, Native American activists carried signs in protest of the inappropriate use of their symbols by Anglos. Symbols have the power to both unite followers and divide groups into "us" and "them." They also can be interpreted as symbolic of past and continued oppression.

A symbol is anything (words, gesture, or object) that carries a particular meaning for the members of a group. A raised finger (which one is important), a green light, a whistle, a handshake, and a raised fist are all symbols with meaning. Some symbols, such as a wink, are trivial, others, like the flag of the United States, are vitally important.

A group's symbols serve two fundamental purposes—they bind together the individual members of a group, and they separate one group from another. Each of the thousands of street gangs in the United States, for example, has a group identity that is displayed in its name, code words, gestures, distinctive clothing, and colors. The symbols of these gangs promote solidarity and set them apart from rivals. These symbols are so important that the members may risk their lives in their defense.[1]

Using symbols to achieve solidarity and community is a common group practice, as the French sociologist Émile Durkheim showed in his classic analysis of primitive religions.[2] Durkheim noted that preliterate people in a locality believed that they were related to some totem, which was usually an animal but could be some other natural object as well. All members of a common group were identified by their shared symbol, which they displayed as the emblem of their totem. This identification with an animal, a bird, or another object is common in U.S. schools. Students, former students, faculty members, and others who identify with the school adopt nicknames for the school's teams, display the school colors, wave the school banner, wear special clothing and jewelry, and engage in ritual chants and songs. These behaviors usually center around athletic contests. Sociologist Janet Lever connects these activities with Durkheim's notion of totemism:

> Team worship, like animal worship, makes all participants intensely aware of their own group membership. By accepting that a particular team represents them symbolically, people enjoy ritual kinship based on a common bond. Their emblem, be it an insignia or a lapel pin or a scarf with team colors, distinguishes fellow fans from both strangers and enemies.[3]

A school's nickname is much more than a tag or a label. It conveys, symbolically as Durkheim suggests, the characteristics and attributes that define the institution. In an important way, the school's symbols represent the institution's self-concept. Schools may have names that signify the school's ethnic heritage (e.g., the Bethany College Swedes), state history (University of Oklahoma Sooners), religion (Oklahoma Baptist College Prophets), or founder (Whittier College Poets). Most schools, though, use symbols of aggression and ferocity for their athletic teams (birds such as hawks, animals such as bulldogs, human categories such as pirates, and even the otherworldly such as devils).[4]

Although school names and other symbols evoke strong emotions of solidarity among followers, there is also a potential dark side to their use. The names, mascots, logos, and flags chosen by some schools may be derogatory to some group. The symbols may dismiss, differentiate, demean, and trivialize marginalized groups such as African Americans, Native Americans, and women. Thus they serve to maintain the dominant status of powerful groups and subordinate those groups categorized as "others." That may not have been the intent of those who decided on the particular names and mascots for a particular school, but their use diminishes these "others," thus retaining the racial and gender inequities found in the larger society.[5] School symbols as used in sports, then, have power, not only for maintaining in-group solidarity, but also for separating the in-group from the out-group and perpetuating the hierarchy between them. Three conspicuous examples of this phenomenon are the use of the Confederate flag at the University of Mississippi, the use of Native American names (Redskins, Scalpers) and other symbols (war paint, tomahawks, Native American dances), and the sexist names given to women's athletic teams.

❦ Symbols of the Confederacy

At Nathan Bedford Forrest High School in Jacksonville, Florida, young African-American athletes wear the Confederate army's colors on their uniforms. They call themselves the Rebels. And the school they play for is named after the slavetrading Confederate general who became the original grand wizard of the Ku Klux Klan.[6]

There is a neo-Confederate culture in much of the South.[7] There are organizations dedicated to promoting the heritage of the Confederate States of America. They fight to retain Confederate symbols, like the Rebel battle flag, that have had a prominent place in many Southern states, most notably Alabama, Georgia, South Carolina, and Mississippi. The neo-Confederate culture and its symbols have two distinct meanings—one that promotes the South's heritage and another that symbolizes slavery, racial separation, and hate.

The Rebel battle flag, which some individuals and groups feel should still fly over state buildings, is an object of controversy. Several states have abandoned it after considerable struggle, but South Carolina continues to have the Rebel flag as its official flag.

The University of Mississippi displays the Rebel battle flag and sings "Dixie" at football games.[8] The practice began in 1948 after the Dixiecrats, rebelling against a strong civil rights plank in the Democratic platform, walked out of the Democratic convention. In that year the University of Mississippi adopted the Rebel flag, designated "Dixie" the school's fight song, and introduced a mascot named "Uncle Reb," a caricature of an Old South plantation owner. These symbols proclaimed its support for racial segregation (its sports teams were officially designated the Rebels in 1936). In 1962 James Meredith, despite the strong opposition of Governor Ross Barnett and other white leaders in the state, became the first black student at the school. There were demonstrations at that time that supported the governor and demonstrations that opposed the racial integration of the school. Through it all, the Rebel flag and the singing of "Dixie" were symbols of defiance used by the supporters of segregation.

Over the ensuing years, the use of these symbols at the University of Mississippi caused considerable debate. On the one hand, they represented the state's heritage and as such were a source of pride, inspiration, and unity among citizens of the South. The opposing position was that these symbols represented a history of oppression against African Americans, noting that the Rebel flag was also a prominent symbol of the Ku Klux Klan. Since almost one-third of Mississippians are African Americans (among the states, Mississippi has the nation's largest African-American population), the flagship university of that state should not use symbols that recall the degradation and demeaning of their ancestors. Is it proper, they ask, to use the key symbol of the Confederacy and African-American enslavement as a rallying symbol for the University of Mississippi's sports teams—teams composed of whites and African Americans?

As a compromise, in 1983, twenty-one years after the University of Mississippi integrated, its chancellor ruled that the Rebel flag was no longer the official banner for the school. Chancellor Porter L. Fortune Jr. made it clear, however, that students would have the right to wave the flag at football games. And that they have done. Sports team names such as "Rebels," as well as mascots such as "Uncle Reb" and songs such as "Dixie," have continued as official school symbols.

In 1997 the debate still raged. Use of the Rebel flag was opposed by the student government and the football coach, Tommy Tuberville, who urged fans to use a less divisive banner (one bearing the letter M studded with stars). Coach Tuberville, by the way, felt that the use of the flag was making it difficult for him to recruit blue-chip African-American players. To his dismay, however, there were groups organized to promote the use of the Rebel flag. "Under the racially charged heading 'Stop the Lynching of Ole Miss and Southern Heritage,' a Jackson, Mississippi, citizens' group recently sent out a mailing, with a Confederate flag on the envelope, asking for money to support its cause."[9] At games, Rebel flags vastly outnumber the Battle M flags. "If anything, the dispute over the university's symbols seems to make many whites more, not less, inclined to cling to the past."[10]

Charles W. Eagles, a University of Mississippi history professor, sums up the ongoing debate:

> For some of us—those who believe in the University of Mississippi—the symbols prevent the university from being everything it can be. Others—those that are faithful to Ole Miss [the traditionalists]—think that if you took the symbols away, there wouldn't be anything there. The symbols are seen as a real burden for the University. But they're the backbone of Ole Miss.

This debate demonstrates vividly the power of symbols, not only the power to unite or divide but also the hold these symbols have on people, as seen in their resistance to change and in the organized efforts to change those symbols interpreted as negative.

◉ The Use of Native American Names and Ceremonial Acts

Ray Franks did an exhaustive study of the names of athletic teams at all U.S. community colleges, colleges, and universities. He found that names associated with Native Americans predominated in popular use.[12] The actual number is not known, but Native American names probably dominate the nation's high school teams as well. Major professional teams have also adopted Native American names—in baseball, the Atlanta Braves and the Cleveland Indians; in football, the Washington Redskins and the Kansas City Chiefs; in basketball, the Golden State Warriors; and in hockey, the Chicago Blackhawks.

Native American names used for sports teams can be generic (Bryant College Indians, Rio Grande College Redmen), tribal (Florida State Seminoles, University of Alaska at Fairbanks Nanooks, Central Michigan Chippewas, Eastern Michigan Hurons, Mississippi College Choctaws, Utah Utes), or they can focus on some attribute (Bradley Braves, Marquette Warriors, Lamar High School [Colorado] Savages) or some combination (University of Illinois Fighting Illini, North Dakota Fighting Sioux).[13]

Defenders of Native American names, logos, and mascots argue that their use is a tribute to the indigenous peoples. Native Americans, the argument goes, are portrayed as brave, resourceful, and strong. Native American names were chosen for sports teams precisely because they represent these positive traits.

Other defenders claim that the use of Native American names and mascots is no different from the use of names and mascots that represent other ethnic groups, such as the Irish or the Vikings or the Norse. Because members of these ethnic groups accept the use of their names, Native Americans should also be proud of this recognition of their heritage.

But Native Americans do object to their symbols being used by athletic teams. Since the early 1970s individuals and organizations such as the American Indian Movement have sought to eliminate the use of Native American names, mascots, and logos by sports teams.[14] They use several key arguments, foremost, racist stereotyping. Names such as Indians, Braves, and Chiefs are not inherently offensive, but some names, logos, and mascots project a violent caricature of Native Americans (scalpers, savages). Teams that use Native American names commonly employ the tomahawk chop, war paint, and mascots dressed as Native Americans. This depiction of Native Americans as bloodthirsty warriors distorts history, since whites invaded Native American lands, oppressed Native peoples, and even employed and justified a policy of genocide toward them.

Some mascots are especially demeaning to Native Americans. Chief Nok-a-homa of the Atlanta Braves comes out of a teepee after an Atlanta homerun and does a ceremonial dance. Many view this as acceptable. But what if the Atlanta team were the Darkies and after a homerun a person looking like a rural black man would come out of a tarpaper shack and pick cotton? Chances are everyone would consider this depiction of another racial group offensive. So too would naming a team Niggers, Spics, or Gooks. Then there is Chief Wahoo, "the red-faced, big-nosed, grinning, drywall-toothed moron who graces the peak of every Cleveland Indians cap."[15] Is such a caricature appropriate? Clyde Bellecourt, national director of the American Indian Movement (AIM), summarizes the complaints:

> If you look up the word "redskin" in both the Webster's and Random House dictionaries, you'll find the word is defined as being offensive. Can you imagine if they called them the Washington Jews and the team mascot was a rabbi leading them in (the song) *Hava Nagila,* fans in the stands wearing yarmulkes and waving little sponge torahs? The word Indian isn't offensive. Brave isn't offensive, but it's the behavior that accompanies all of this that's offensive. The rubber tomahawks. The chicken-feather headdresses. People wearing war paint and making these ridiculous war whoops with a toma-

hawk in one hand and a beer in the other. All of these things have significant meaning for us. And the psychological impact it has, especially on our youth, is devastating.[16]

Another problem is the imitation or misuse of symbols that have religious significance to some Native American peoples. Using dances, chants, drummings, and other rituals at sporting events clearly trivializes their meaning.

Also problematic is the homogenization of Native American cultures. Native Americans are portrayed uniformly, without regard for the sometimes enormous differences among tribes. Thus, through the use of Native American names of mascots, society defines who Native Americans are instead of allowing Native Americans to determine how society thinks of them.

A few colleges, such as Stanford, Siena, Miami of Ohio, Dartmouth, and St. John's, have taken these objections seriously and have changed their names and mascots. Most high schools and colleges, however, resist such a change. Ironically, they insist on retaining the Native American symbols even though those schools do not have a Native American heritage or significant Native American student representation. The members of these schools and their constituencies insist on retaining their Native American names because they are part of their collective identities. This allegiance to their school symbols seems to have higher priority than sensitivity to the negative consequences produced by inappropriate depictions of Native Americans.

❧ Sexist Names for Women's Teams[17]

Many studies have shown the varied ways in which language acts in the defining, deprecation, and exclusion of women.[18] Names do this, too. Naming women's and men's athletic team is not a neutral process. The names chosen often are badges of femininity and masculinity, hence of inferiority and superiority. To the degree that this occurs, the names of women's and men's athletic teams reinforce a basic element of social structure: gender division and hierarchy. Team names reflect this division as well as the asymmetry that is associated with it. Despite advances made by women in sport since the implementation of Title IX, widespread naming practices continue to mark female athletes as unusual, aberrant, or invisible.

My colleague Maxine Baca Zinn and I examined the names and accompanying logos and mascots of sports teams for women and men at 1,185 coeducational four-year colleges and universities.[19] We identified eight gender-linked practices associated with names/logos that diminish and trivialize women.

First, physical markers. One common naming practice emphasizes the physical appearance of women, such as the Angelo State Rambelles, or the Bellarmine College Belles (the men are the Knights). As Casey Miller and Kate Swift argue, this practice is sexist because the "emphasis on the physical characteristics of women is offensive in contexts where men are described in terms of achievement."[20]

Second, girl or gal. The use of "girl" or "gal" stresses the presumed immaturity and irresponsibility of women, such as the Elon College Golden Girls. "Just as *boy* can be blatantly offensive to minority men, so *girl* can have comparable patronizing and demeaning implications for women."[21]

Third, feminine suffixes. This is a popular form of gender differentiation found in the names of athletic, social, and women's groups. The practice not only marks women but also denotes a feminine derivative by establishing a "female negative trivial category."[22] The devaluation is accomplished by tagging words with feminine suffixes such as "ette." At Dillard University the men's team is the Blue Devils, and the women's team is the Devilettes; at Albany State the men are the Golden Rams and the women are the Rammettes. Another suffix is "esse." At Duquesne University and James Madison University the men are the Dukes and the women the Duchesses.

Fourth, lady. This label has several meanings that demean women as athletes. Lady is used to "evoke a standard of propriety, correct behavior, and elegance,"[23] characteristics that are decidedly unathletic. Similarly, "lady" carries overtones recalling the age of chivalry. "This makes the term seem polite at first, but we must also remember that these implications are perilous: they suggest that a 'lady' is helpless, and cannot do things for herself."[24] The use of "lady" for women's teams is common, for example, the University of Florida Lady Gators or the University of Arkansas Lady Razorbacks. At Kenyon College the men are the Lords and the women the Ladies, and at Washington and Jefferson College the men are Presidents and the women, First Ladies. In both of these instances the names for the women's teams clearly mark their status as inferior to that of the men.

Fifth, male as a false generic. This practice assumes that the masculine in the language, word, or name choice is the norm while ignoring the feminine altogether. Miller and Swift define this procedure as "terms used of a class or group that are not applicable to all members."[25] The use of "mankind" to encompass both sexes has its parallel among men's and women's athletic teams that have the same name, for example, the Rams (Colorado State University), Stags (Concordia College), Norsemen (Luther College), the Tomcats (Thiel College), and the Hokies (a hokie is a castrated turkey; Virginia Tech). Dale Spender has called the practice of treating the masculine as the norm "one of the most pervasive and pernicious rules that has been encoded."[26] Its consequence is to make women invisible as well as secondary to men, since they are robbed of a separate identity.

Sixth, male name with a female modifier. This practice applies the feminine to a name that usually denotes a male, giving females lower status.[27] Examples among sports teams are the Lady Friars of Providence College, the Lady Statesmen of William Penn College, the Lady Penmen of New Hampshire College, the Lady Centaurs of Columbia College, and the Lady Gamecocks of the University of South Carolina (a gamecock is a fighting rooster). Using such oxymorons "reflects role conflict and contributes to the lack of acceptance of women's sport."[28]

Seventh, double gender marking. This occurs when the name of the women's team is a diminutive of the men's team name combined with "belle" or "lady" or other feminine modifier. For example, the men's teams at Mississippi College are the Choctaws, and the women's teams are designated as the Lady Chocs. At the University of Kentucky the men's teams are the Wildcats and the women's teams are the Lady Kats. The men's teams at the University of Colorado are the Buffalos and the women's teams are the Lady Buffs. At Augusta College the women are the Lady Jags, whereas the men are the Jaguars. Similarly, at both the University of Nebraska–Omaha and the University of Texas–Arlington, the men are the Mavericks and the women, the Lady Mavs. Compounding the feminine intensifies women's secondary status. Double gender marking occurs "perhaps to underline the inappropriateness or rarity of the feminine noun or to emphasize its negativity."[29]

Eighth, male/female paired polarity. Women's and men's teams can be assigned names that represent a female/male opposition. When this occurs, the names of the men's teams embody competitiveness and other positive traits associated with sport, whereas the names for women's teams are lighthearted or cute. The essence of sport is competition, and physical skills largely determine outcomes. Successful athletes are believed to embody such traits as courage, bravura, boldness, self-confidence, and aggression. When the names given men's teams imply these traits but the names for women's teams suggest that women are playful and cuddly, then women are trivialized and de-athleticized. For example, the College of Wooster men are the Fighting Scots, and the women are the Scotties; Mercer University men's teams are the Bears and the women are the Teddy Bears; at the Albany College of Pharmacy the men are the Panthers and the women, the Pink Panthers; and at Fort Valley State College the men's teams are named the Wildcats and the women's teams, the Wildkittens.

Another grouping occurs when names that could be included in one of the above categories also incorporate race. This occurs especially with teams using Native American symbols. The men's teams at Southeastern Oklahoma State University are the Savages and the women's teams are the Savagettes, using the diminutive feminine suffix combined with a negative stereotype for the racial category. Similarly, at Montclair State College the men are the Indians and the women are the Squaws. The word "squaw" also refers to a woman's pelvic area and means prostitute in some native languages. Vernon Bellecourt of the American Indian Movement says, "The issue itself is clear. . . . The word 'squaw' has got to go in all its forms. It's demeaning and degrading to Indian women and all women."[30]

Our survey found that approximately three-eighths of U.S. colleges and universities employ sexist names and slightly over half have sexist names and/or logos for their athletic teams. Thus the identity symbols for athletic teams at those schools contribute to the maintenance of male dominance within college sports. Since the traditional masculine gender role matches most athletic qualities better than the traditional feminine gender role, the images and symbols are male. Women do not fit into this scheme. They are "other" even when they do participate. Their team names and logos tend to perpetuate and strengthen the image of female inferiority by making them secondary, invisible, trivial, or unathletic.

❧ Resistance to Change

It is important to note that many schools do not have team names, mascots, and logos that are racist or sexist. They use race-neutral and gender-neutral names such as Bears, Eagles, Seagulls, Cougars, Wasps, Mustangs, Royals, Saints, Big Green, or Blue Streaks. Schools that currently employ racist or sexist names could change to neutral ones that embody the traits desired in athletic teams such as courage, strength, and aggressiveness.[31] For some, such a change would be relatively easy—dropping the use of "lady" or "ette" as modifiers, for example. Teams with Native American names or male names (stags, rams, hokies, centaurs) must adopt new names to eliminate the racism or sexism inherent in their present names. A few schools have made these changes over the past fifteen years or so. Most schools, however, resist changing names with passion because a name change negates the school's traditions.

The athletic teams at my school, Colorado State University, are called the Rams. Is it appropriate for the women's teams to be called Rams (rams are male sheep)? This question has been raised from time to time by the Faculty Women's Caucus and a few male professors, but strong resistance from journalists, student government leaders, and the Committee on Intercollegiate Athletics, as well as silence by the women athletes and the coaches of women's teams, have worked to maintain the status quo.

The naming issue at Colorado State University reveals a contradiction. Many students, including women student-athletes, express a lack of interest in the issue, yet it evokes strong emotions among others. These responses seem to originate in several sources at Colorado State and, by implication, elsewhere. These arguments parallel resistance to changing sexist language in general.[32]

Tradition, above all, is always a barrier to change. Students, alumni, faculty, and athletes become accustomed to a particular name for their university and its athletic teams, and it seems "natural." This is the argument made on behalf of the many teams that continue to use Native American names and symbols for their teams despite the objections of Native Americans. So too with names that are sexist, But even if a school name has the force of tradition, is it justified to continue using it if it is racist or sexist? If a sexist team name reinforces and socializes sexist thinking, however subtly, then it must be changed. If not, then the institution is publicly sexist.

Many see the naming issue as trivial. However, it is not trivial to the group being demeaned, degraded, and trivialized. Some progressives argue that there are more important issues to address than changing racist or sexist names of athletic teams. This illustrates the contradiction that the naming of teams is at once trivial and important. For African Americans, whether the University of Mississippi fans sing "Dixie" and wave Confederate flags is not as important as ending discrimination and getting good jobs. Similarly, for Native Americans the derogatory use of their heritage surrounding athletic contests is relatively unimportant compared to raising their standard of living. For women, the sexist naming of athletic teams is not as significant as pay equity or breaking the "glass ceiling" or achieving equity with men in athletic departments in resources, scholarships, and media attention. Faced with a choice among these options, the naming issue would be secondary. But this sets up a false choice. We can work to remove all manifestations of racism and sexism on college campuses. Referring to language and relevant to the team names issue as well, the Association for Women in Psychology Ad Hoc Committee on Sexist Language has addressed and refuted the "trivial concern" argument:

> The major objection, often even to *discussing* changing sexist language, is that it is a superficial matter compared with the real physical and economic oppression of women. And indeed, women's total oppression must end; we are not suggesting any diversion of energies from that struggle. We are, however, suggesting that this is an important part of it.[33]

The opposite point—that the naming issue is crucially important—is the third argument. Symbols are extremely compelling in the messages they convey. Their importance is understood when rebellious groups demean or defame symbols of the powerful, such as the flag. Names and other symbols have the power to elevate or "put down" a group. If racist or sexist, they reinforce and therefore maintain the secondary status of African Americans, Native Americans, or women through stereotyping, caricature, derogation, trivialization, diminution, or making them invisible. Most of us, however, fail to see the problem with symbols that demean or defame the powerless because these symbols support the existing power arrangements in society. Despite their apparent triviality, the symbols surrounding sports teams are important because they can (and often do) contribute to patterns of social dominance.

Colleges and universities, for the most part, are making major efforts to diversify their student bodies, faculties, and administrations by race, ethnicity, and gender. This laudable goal is clearly at odds with the existence of racist and sexist names and practices for their athletic teams. The leadership in these schools (boards of regents, chancellors, presidents, and faculty senates) must take a stand against racism and sexism in all its forms and take appropriate action. Removing all racist and sexist symbols such as names, mascots, flags, logos, and songs is an important beginning to this crucial project.

Endnotes

[1]See, for example, Martin Sanchez Jankowski, *Islands in the Street: Gangs and American Urban Society* (Berkeley: University of California Press, 1991).

[2]Emile Durkheim, *The Elementary Forms of Religious Life,* trans. Joseph Ward Sivain (New York: Free Press, 1947). This classic was first published in 1915.

[3]Janet Lever, *Soccer Madness* (Chicago: University of Chicago Press, 1983), p. 12.

[4]See John R. Fuller and Elisabeth Anne Manning, "Violence and Sexism in College Mascots and Symbols: A Typology," *Free Inquiry in Creative Sociology* 15 (1987): 61–64.

[5]Margaret Carlisle Duncan, "Representation and the Gun That Points Backwards," *Journal of Sport and Social Issues* 17 (April 1993): 42–46.

[6]Dennis Cauchon, "A Slave-Holding Past: Search for Perspective," *USA Today,* March 9, 1998, p. 8A.

[7]Brian Britt, "Neo-Confederate Culture," *Z Magazine* 9 (December 1996): 26–30.

[8]The following is taken from three sources: William Nack, "Look Away, Dixie Land," *Sports Illustrated,* November 3, 1997, p. 114; Douglas S. Lederman, "Old Times Not Forgotten: A Battle Over Symbols," in *Sport in Contemporary Society,* ed. D. Stanley Eitzen, 5th ed. (New York: St. Martin's, 1996), pp. 128–133; and Paula Edelson, "Just Whistlin' Dixie," *Z Magazine* 4 (November 1991): 72–74.

[9]Nack, "Look Away."

[10]Lederman, "Old Times Not Forgotten," p. 132.

[11]Ibid., p. 133.

[12]Ray Franks, *What's in a Nickname? Exploring the Jungle of College Athletic Mascots* (Amarillo, Tex.: Ray Franks, 1982).

[13]The names and mascots for schools used in this essay are taken from Ray Franks, *What's in a Nickname?* This comprehensive compilation of information, although dated, is the most current listing. Therefore, some of the schools named in the essay may have subsequently changed the names of their athletic teams.

[14]This section is taken primarily from two sources: Laurel Davis, "Protest against the Use of Native American Mascots: A Challenge to Traditional American Identity," *Journal of Sport and Social Issues* 17 (April 1993): 9–22; and Ward Churchill, "Crimes against Humanity," *Sport in Contemporary Society,* ed. D. Stanley Eitzen, 5th ed. (New York: St. Martin's, 1996), pp. 134–141.

[15]Rick Telander, "These Nicknames, Symbols Should Offend All Americans," *Chicago Sun-Times,* October 20, 1995, p. 143.

[16]Quoted in Bob Kravitz, "Aim of Native Americans' Protest Is True," *Rocky Mountain News,* January 21, 1992, p. 39.

[17]This section is based in part on D. Stanley Eitzen and Maxine Baca Zinn, "The De-Athleticization of Women: The Naming and Gender Marking of Collegiate Sport Teams," *Sociology of Sport Journal* 6 (December 1989): 362–370; D. Stanley Eitzen and Maxine Baca Zinn, "The Sexist Naming of Athletic Teams and Resistance to Change," *Journal of Sport and Social Issues* 17 (April 1993): 34–41; D. Stanley Eitzen and Maxine Baca Zinn, "Never Mind the Braves; What about the Lady Rams?" *Baltimore Sun,* November 3, 1991, p. 3D.

[18]Barrie Thorne, Cheris Kramarae, and Nancy M. Henley, "Language, Gender, and Society: Opening a Second Decade of Research," in *Language, Gender, and Society,* ed. Barrie Thorne and Nancy M. Henley (Rowley, Mass.: Newbury House, 1985), pp. 7–24; Nancy M. Henley, "This New Species That Seeks a New Language: On Sexism in Language and Language Change," in *Women and Men in Transition,* ed. Joyce Penfield (Albany: State University of New York Press, 1987), pp. 3–27.

[19]Eitzen and Baca Zinn, "Sexist Naming of Athletic Teams."

[20]Casey Miller and Kate Swift, *The Handbook of Nonsexist Writing* (New York: Lippincott and Crowell, 1980), p. 87.

[21]Ibid., p. 71.

[22]Casey Miller and Kate Swift, *Words and Women: New Language in New Times* (Garden City, N.Y.: Doubleday-Anchor, 1977), p. 58.

[23]Ibid., p. 72.

[24]Robin Lakoff, *Language and Woman's Place* (New York: Harper and Row, 1975), p. 25.

[25]Miller and Swift, *Handbook of Nonsexist Writing,* p. 9.

[26]Dale Spender, *Man Made Language* (London: Routledge and Kegan Paul, 1980), p. 3.

[27]Dennis Baron, *Grammar and Gender* (New Haven: Yale University Press, 1986), p. 112.

[28]Fuller and Manning, "Violence and Sexism," p. 64.

[29]Baron, *Grammar and Gender,* p. 115.

[30]Quoted in Lois Tomas, "What's in a Name?" *In These Times,* October 19, 1997, p. 11.

[31]Daniel P. Starr, "Unisex Nicknames One Way of Skirting Gender Problem," *NCAA News,* March 20, 1991, p. 4.

[32]Maija S. Blaubergs, "An Analysis of Classic Arguments against Changing Sexist Language," *Women's Studies International Quarterly* 3 (1980): 135–147.

[33]Association for Women in Psychology Ad Hoc Committee on Sexist Language, "Help Stamp Out Sexism: Change the Language!" *APA Monitor* 6, no. 11 (1975): 16.

❧ ❧ ❧

Questions

1. How can the use of logos and mascots simultaneously bind members of a group together yet separate groups?

2. Of the three classes of mascots and logos discussed by Eitzen (confederate south, Native Americans, and women), which do you think has the potential to be most damaging for oppressed members of society? Why?

3. What are the eight gender-related practices commonly used when naming school athletic teams?

4. Why does there seem to be so much resistance to changing athletic team names, logos, and mascots?

5. Look over your own schooling and/or athletic team experiences from middle school to present. How prevalent is the use of negative stereotypes, logos, or mascots in your own community? How much of a negative effect do you think these mascots and logos have had in your community?

White Racism: A Sociology of Human Waste

JOE R. FEAGIN AND HERNÁN VERA

The concept of white racism has become more controversial in recent years, especially as a growing number of college campuses offer courses with this specific title. However, there is very little understanding of what the concept actually means, let alone how it differs from "racism" in general. In this article, Joe R. Feagin and Hernán Vera focus on the human costs of white racism for blacks and for society as a whole. What can we do to solve this social problem?

*W*hite racism is one of the most difficult problems facing the United States today and is the most consequential for the nation's future. White racism has the potential to array white and black Americans against each other in ways that could eventually devastate the social and political structure of the United States. Witness the events of the 1990s in the former Yugoslavia or Soviet Union, where members of ethnic factions have killed one another with less apparent justification than some black victims of recurring racism might have to lash out violently against their white oppressors.

The days of urban rebellion in Los Angeles in the spring of 1992, when some African and Latino Americans did lash out at a cost of many lives and vast property damage, provide but one example of the violent consequences of racial oppression. Anger and rage at white racism lay behind the Los Angeles uprising and the many other black rebellions that have taken place since the 1930s. Referring to the likelihood of additional urban uprisings following the Los Angeles riot, Housing and Urban Development (HUD) Secretary Henry Cisneros argued that "like piles of dry wood with red-hot coals underneath, scores of American cities can ignite" because of America's "dirty secret": racism.[1] . . .

Traditional discussions often treat the system called white racism as a zero-sum game of power and resources, a view that assumes a scarcity of critical societal resources for which racial groups inevitably contend. We depart from this narrow perspective and argue for the existence of a surplus of societal resources and human talents that white racism allows to be routinely squandered and dissipated. On reflection, many whites can recognize some of the waste of black talent and resources brought about by discriminatory barriers, but few realize how great this loss is for African Americans. Even fewer whites realize the huge amount of energy and talent that whites themselves have dissipated in their construction of antiblack attitudes and ideologies and in their participation in racial discrimination. . . . We believe that U.S. society is paying a heavy price in material, psychological, and moral terms for the persistence of white-generated racism.

Racial relations scholar bell hooks argues that approaches emphasizing the hurt whites experience from racism risk "obscuring the particular ways racist domination impacts on the lives of marginalized groups," for many people "benefit greatly from dominating others and are not suffering a wound that is in any way similar to the condition of the exploited and oppressed."[2] We agree that the costs are far greater for the oppressed. Our argument about the costly character of racism recognizes that black and other minority victims of racial oppression typically pay a *direct, heavy, and immediately painful* price for racism, while white discriminators and onlookers usually pay a *more indirect and seldom recognized* price. In addition, for whites the benefits accruing from racism to a varying degree offset the negative consequences. Clearly the net cost of racism is not equal across racial groups, but nonetheless the cost for all is great. . . .

❧ Denying the Reality of White Racism

Until civil rights laws were passed during the Lyndon Johnson administration in the 1960s, most African Americans faced blatant discrimination that was legally prescribed or permitted. Few had the resources to vigorously counter this racism, and the legal system offered little support. In the years following the civil rights revolution, as state-enforced segregation was demolished, many felt optimistic about the future. Black people began moving into many formerly forbidden areas of U.S. society, and whites began to encounter a greater black presence in historically white public facilities, workplaces, businesses, churches, schools, and neighborhoods.

However, the civil rights revolution came to a standstill in the 1980s, and many African Americans now believe that the country and its government are moving backward in the quest for racial justice.[3] Presidential use of the White House as a "bully pulpit" for conservative political agendas during the Reagan and Bush years of the 1980s and early 1990s was particularly devastating to racial relations. Federal civil rights enforcement programs were weakened significantly in this period. The political denial of white racism made its way into intellectual circles and the mass media, where the concept of the "declining significance of race" became fashionable. Since the mid-1970s many influential commentators and authors have argued or implied that white racism is no longer a serious, entrenched national problem and that African Americans must take total responsibility for their own individual and community problems.

A majority of white Americans in all social classes, including jurists, scholars, and commentators, now appear to believe that serious racism is declining in the United States; that black Americans have made great civil rights progress in recent decades; and that blacks should be content with that progress. Whites see widespread discrimination in most institutional arenas as a thing of the past. In particular, many whites believe that the black middle class no longer faces significant discrimination and is thriving economically—indeed more so than the white middle class. Whites typically view problems of the black underclass as the central issue for black America and believe that that class's condition has little to do with discrimination. . . . The white notion that any black person who works hard enough can succeed is even reflected in white reactions to the Bill Cosby show described by researchers Sut Jhally and Justin Lewis. Many whites felt the series, which portrayed a successful black upper-middle-class family and became the highest-rated sitcom on national television during the 1980s, showed a "world where race no longer matters." Jhally and Lewis noted that this view of the show enabled whites to "combine an impeccably liberal attitude toward race with a deep-rooted suspicion of black people."[4] . . .

☙ The Reality of Racism

The substantial white consensus on the decline of racism is not based on empirical evidence. On the contrary, research shows that black men and women still face extensive racial discrimination in all arenas of daily life. . . . Recent in-depth studies have documented continuing antiblack discrimination, ranging from blatant acts reminiscent of the legal segregation period to subtle and covert forms that have flourished under the conditions of desegregation. The belief in the declining significance of race cannot be reconciled with the empirical reality of racial discrimination. Great anger over white racism can be found today in every socioeconomic group of black Americans, from millionaires to day laborers.[5]

White supremacy groups have been at the forefront of attackers of African Americans. Membership in the Ku Klux Klan, the largest white supremacy group for most of the twentieth century, reached five million in the 1920s. After a period of decline, Klan membership began to grow again in the 1970s, and in the early 1990s the number of white Americans in various Klan factions was estimated at about

10,000. Newspaper reports have documented Klan violence against minorities and have described paramilitary training camps designed to prepare Klan members for a "race war." From the 1970s to the 1990s, the Klan and other white supremacy groups have been involved in hundreds of antiblack and anti Jewish attacks; several members of such groups have been convicted of murdering or assaulting black people.[6] Other white supremacy groups such as the White Aryan Resistance (WAR), headed by white supremacist Tom Metzger, . . . have emerged in recent years. One nationwide count found more than 300 hate groups active in 1992, ranging from skinheads to a variety of neo-Nazi and other white supremacy organizations. White supremacy groups in the United States have been estimated to have at least 30,000 hard-core members, with perhaps another 200,000 active sympathizers.[7]

During the 1980s and 1990s hundreds of acts of vandalism and intimidation were directed at black and other minority Americans. One of the most notorious incidents occurred in 1986 in the Howard Beach area of New York City, when three black men were beaten and chased by white youths. One of the men died when he was chased into the path of a car. A few days later 5,000 people, black and white, marched through Howard Beach to protest the attack.[8] In 1991 alone, 25 hate-motivated murders of minority Americans by white killers were recorded in the United States. Many other hate killings undoubtedly went unreported. In one recent incident, two white men went on a rampage in a Washington, D.C. suburb. They were looking for black pedestrians to attack. They ended their night by tearing the clothes off a black woman and calling her "nigger."[9] In 1993 two white men were convicted in south Florida of the kidnapping, robbery, and attempted murder of a black stockbrokerage clerk who was vacationing in Tampa. The black man was set ablaze by the whites, who left a note saying, "One less nigger, more to go."[10]

Hate crimes targeting African Americans represent only the tip of the racist iceberg. Black people also continue to face discrimination in the workplace, in business, in colleges, in public accommodations, and in historically white neighborhoods. Millions of cases of discrimination occur each year. More than half of the black respondents in a 1989 ABC News survey agreed that black workers generally faced discrimination when seeking skilled jobs; 61% gave a similar reply regarding managerial jobs.[11] A 1991 Urban Institute report presented a study in which white and black applicants with similar qualifications were sent to the same employers to apply for jobs; a significant proportion of the black applicants suffered discrimination in the hiring process.[12] Even if a black applicant is hired, discriminatory barriers are likely to impair career progress. Racial discrimination continues to handicap African Americans today in all major institutional arenas of our society.[13] . . .

Persisting racial inequality can also be seen in the wide gaps in black and white family income and wealth. Today the median income of black families is about 58% that of white families. Blacks are almost three times as likely to live in poverty as are whites, and the median net worth of black families is less than 10% that of white families.[14] These data underscore the long-term advantages of being white in this society. Young white Americans sometimes argue that they have not personally held slaves or discriminated against black people and therefore should not have to pay the price of remedies for racial discrimination. However, this argument fails to take into account the many ways in which young whites have benefited from their forebears' access to land, decent-paying jobs, and wealth at a time when most African Americans were excluded from those things. Two decades of modest government remedial programs like Affirmative Action have not offset several hundred years of white advantage. Although the economic benefits of white privilege have gone in disproportionately large amounts to the employer class, all white groups derive at least some psychological benefit from having a group below them, from the feeling of superiority that is especially important for whites who are not doing well economically. . . .

❀ A New Theory:
Racism as Societal Waste

White racism can be viewed as the socially organized set of attitudes, ideas, and practices that deny African Americans and other people of color the dignity, opportunities, freedoms, and rewards that this nation offers white Americans. The concept of white racism encompasses the attitudes and ideologies that motivate negative actions against blacks and other minorities. Racist acts have ranged from overt extermination and murder, to subtle gestures of social exclusion, to passive acquiescence in the racist acts of others. Typically, racist acts and practices are institutionalized; they are embedded in and shaped by social contexts. These practices have sometimes been defined as illegal under U.S. law. This is the case for certain types of blatant employment, educational, and housing discrimination that fall under the 1964 and 1968 civil rights acts. . . .

Viewed in broad terms, white racist practices represent socially sanctioned ways of dissipating much human talent and energy. . . .

. . . Americans should see white racism for what it actually is: a tremendously wasteful set of practices, legitimated by deeply embedded myths, that deprives its victims, its perpetrators, and U.S. society as a whole of much valuable human talent and energy and many social, economic, and political resources.

❀ Racism as Ritual

Social practices that dissipate human resources and energies are often ritualized, that is, they are routine and recurring actions distinguished by symbolic meanings that pervade and guide their performance. Recent social science research has paid surprisingly little attention to the ritual nature of racist events, although general observers have occasionally noted the ceremonial and formalized character of U.S. racial relations. Note, for example, the following comment made by Lillian Smith, a white Southerner, during the era of legal segregation: "For we [whites] used those lynchings as a symbolic rite to keep alive in men's minds the idea of white supremacy, and we set up a system of avoidance rites that destroyed not bodies but the spirit of men."[15] We find the imagery of rites and rituals useful in analyzing racism in U.S. society. The concrete events and actions of racism frequently have a ritual nature. Racist rites involve minority victims, several categories of white participants (officiants, acolytes, and passive observers), a range of acts (gestures, words, avoidance, physical attacks), an assortment of instruments (workplace appraisal forms, burning crosses, police batons), and an array of myths (stereotypes about black Americans) that legitimate racist acts in perpetrators' minds. . . .

By the use of physical, psychological, or symbolic force racist rituals deprive their victims of fundamental human rights and destroy talents, energy, and lives. The millions of people of color in the United States who have been and continue to be sacrificed to the mythological needs of white superiority are in certain ways like the sacrificial victims in the religious rites of some ancient societies: alien others who may be compelled to forfeit their lives or well-being in the name of compelling dominant-group interests. The targets of racism vary in their ability to redress their abuse. Those who are poor . . . generally do not have the power and resources to counter discrimination that are available to middle-class victims. . . .

. . .

Racial Discrimination and Racial Mythology

One active part of racism, discrimination, has rarely been defined in the social science literature. For example, in *An American Dilemma* Gunnar Myrdal noted widespread discrimination in U.S. society but never delimited it. Subsequent researchers of black-white relations have usually not provided a specific definition.[16] Researchers who have ventured on more precise delineations in recent years have emphasized group power and institutionalized factors: for instance, Thomas Pettigrew has suggested that discrimination is "an institutional process of exclusion against an outgroup."[17] Joe R. Feagin and Clairece B. Feagin have defined discrimination as "practices carried out by members of dominant groups which have a differential and negative impact on members of subordinate groups."[18] The crucial point of these definitions is that the ability to carry out significant and repeated discriminatory acts flows from the power one group has over another. In addition, both individual and collective discrimination can occur in an array of locations—in public accommodations, schools and colleges, workplaces, and neighborhoods.

Discriminatory practices are supported by ideological constructions taken on faith. Racial myths are part of the mind-set that helps whites interpret their experience and that influences behavior, alters emotions, and shapes what whites see and do not see.[19] The cognitive notions and stereotypes of contemporary racism, which include myths of the dangerous black man, the lazy black person, the black woman's fondness for welfare, and black inferiority and incompetence, make as little empirical sense as the hostile fictions that underlay the Nazi Holocaust. However, such antiblack fictions are sincerely held by many whites. . . .

The persistence of antiblack discrimination indicates how deeply myths of racial difference and inequality have become embedded in white thinking. Such myths often influence the important decisions that whites make, from selecting a spouse to choosing a residential neighborhood.[20] Yet white views of blacks are often not based on significant personal experience with African Americans. In contrast, black views of whites are much more likely to be grounded in personal experience because most blacks have had substantial experience with whites by the time they are a few years old. In her classic analysis, *Killers of the Dream*, Lillian Smith noted that prejudiced thinking and antiblack practices become "ceremonial," that they "slip from the conscious mind deep into the muscles."[21] These attitudes and propensities are learned at such an early point in a white child's development that they become routinized and unconscious. Smith also pointed out the insidiousness of racial learning in early childhood: "The mother who taught me tenderness . . . taught me the bleak rituals of keeping Negroes in their place."[22]

The stereotyped portrayals of African Americans and the unrealistically sanguine views of contemporary racial relations often presented in the mainstream media help perpetuate the racist myths held by ordinary white Americans. Leonard Berkowitz, among many others, has argued that the mass media play an important role in reinforcing antisocial images and behavior.[23] The U.S. media are overwhelmingly white-oriented and white-controlled. White control of powerful institutions—from the mass media to corporate workplaces to universities to police departments—signals white dominance to all members of the society.

At the individual level, much antiblack discrimination is perpetrated by whites who are not overtly aware of their ingrained prejudices and negative emotions. A white supervisor in the workplace may refuse to hire a black applicant because of the belief that white workers or customers are uncomfortable with people unlike themselves. . . . Even in predominantly white colleges and universities, black students and faculty members are frequently victims of white prejudices, many of which seem buried deep in white consciousness. . . . Whites do not need to be aware of their racial motivations to inflict harm on blacks.

The paradoxical phenomenon of whites who claim not to be racist perpetrating racially harmful acts can be explained in part by the fact that "racism" has come to be held in such opprobrium that few whites are willing to accept "racist" as a personal trait. This marks a change from the past. At an earlier time in U.S. history, even white powerholders paraded their racism as a sign of honor. Employers and politicians publicly joined the Klan in the 1920s and 1930s. Today the powerful may hide or deny their racist attitudes out of fear of disgrace, but racist acts have not ceased. The layers of euphemisms and code words that often cover racist acts today can make it difficult to demonstrate that such acts are in fact intentionally discriminatory.

Racism and the White Self

Racism is a fundamental part of U.S. culture and is spread throughout the social fabric. Because virtually all whites participate in the racist culture, most harbor some racist images or views. At the extreme end of the spectrum are white perpetrators of physically violent racist acts: these whites share with other whites some common antiblack attitudes, but one distinguishing feature is their fixation on blacks. Obsessive racists may use their racial prejudices to resolve deep psychological problems. Many white supremacists seem to fit into this category. At the opposite end of the spectrum, the least obsessive racists may hold traditional antiblack prejudices simply to conform to their social environments.

Racism, however, encompasses more than the way whites view the black "others." It also involves the way whites view themselves as a result of participating in a culturally and structurally racist society. Prejudice, a term that ordinarily refers to negative views of others, can also apply to positive views of oneself or one's own group. Prejudices and related discriminatory practices reflect an internal representation of oneself as well as of the hated other. In the process of developing this self-definition, whites have created a set of "sincere fictions"—personal mythologies that reproduce societal mythologies at the individual level. Whites generally use these fictions to define themselves as "not racist," as "good people," even as they think and act in antiblack ways. It is common for a white person to say, "I am not a racist," often, and ironically, in conjunction with negative comments about people of color. The sincere fictions embedded in white personalities and white society are about both the black other *and* the white self. Long ago Frederick Douglass termed the white fictions about the black other "an old dodge," "for wherever men oppress their fellows, wherever they enslave them, they will endeavor to find the needed apology for such enslavement and oppression in the character of the people oppressed and enslaved."[24]

Among the important fictions about the white self is an internalized conception of "whiteness" that is often deep and hidden in the

104

individual psyche. As Ruth Frankenberg found in interviews with white women, whiteness is "difficult for white people to name. . . . Those who are securely housed within its borders usually do not examine it."[25] Frankenberg also notes that the dimensions of whiteness include not only ways of thinking about the white self but also "ways of understanding history."[26]

. . .

❂ Conclusion

. . .

The mythology of white racism is, at its core, part of a rationalization of the destruction of human talents, energies, and resources. From the individual point of view, ideological racism is one way that whites legitimate the mistreatment of people of color and defend their self-conceptions as actors and observers in antiblack dramas. From the institutional point of view, racism is the social organization of the wasteful expenditure of energy aimed at sacrificing the human talent, potential, and energy of targeted racial groups such as African Americans.

It is important to explore not only the character of the problem of white racism but also solutions for that problem. We noted in the opening of this chapter that a successful antiracist struggle will involve a critical examination of the many sincere fictions undergirding racist action. A dramatic change in individual, group, and societal ways of seeing requires a change in white thinking about the history and reality of racism. Many whites oppose a thoroughgoing destruction of racism because of the zero-sum idea that whites will only lose in the process. This sincere fiction has supported much racial discrimination, but it is inaccurate and destructive. We propose a refocusing of our social vision to closely scrutinize the human propensity to waste excess energy and resources. This change will require a radical reordering of our thinking and, even more importantly, a radical restructuring of our interracial ethics and interpersonal connectedness. We propose that all Americans, but especially white Americans, search for more positive and productive ways of using this society's excess energy and resources. A better utilization of resources currently being wasted by racism will improve the lives of all Americans. Much pessimism has been recently expressed about the possibility of major change in U.S. racial relations, and we understand well why this is the case. Yet we do not share this pessimism. In our lifetimes we have seen major changes in U.S. racial relations, even though many of these changes were forced on whites by minority protest movements. These changes have benefited not only African Americans and other people of color but also white Americans. This nation has changed in the past in the direction of greater racial equality, and it can do so again.

Endnotes

[1]Roberts, S. V. (1993, April 19). Lift every voice and sing—A new song. *U.S. News & World Report.* 8.

[2]hooks, b. (1992). *Black looks.* Boston: South End Press, 13.

[3]See Feagin, J. R., & Sikes, M. P. (1994). *Living with racism: The black middle class experience.* Boston: Beacon; Cose, E. (1993). *The rage of a privileged class.* New York: Harper Collins.

[4]See Jhally, S., & Lewis, J. (1992). *Enlightened racism: The Cosby show, audiences, and the myth of the American dream.* (1992). Boulder, CO: Westview Press, 110.

[5]See Essed, P. (1991). *Understanding everyday racism: An interdisciplinary theory.* Beverly Hills, CA: Sage; Feagin & Sikes, *Living with racism;* and Cose, *The rage of a privileged class.*

[6]Diebel, L. (1992, February 23). Darkest Iowa. *Toronto Star,* p. Fl; Press, A., & Smith, V. (1987, February 23). Going after the Klan, *Newsweek,* 29.

[7]See Ridgeway, J. (1990). *Blood in the face: The Ku Klux Klan, Aryan nations, Nazi Skinheads, and the rise of a new white culture.* New York: Thunder's Mouth Press.

[8]Tension rises in New York in March over black's death. (1986, December 28). *Austin American-Statesman,* A3.

[9]FBI issues first data on hate crimes. (1993, March 15). *Race Relations Reporter*, 8; Debusmann, B. (1992, March 4). Hate crime shocks Washington. Reuters News Service.

[10]Martinez, J. (1993, September 8). Two guilty in racial burning. *Gainesville Sun.*

[11]Sigelman, L., & Welch, S. (1991). *Black Americans' views of racial inequality.* Cambridge: Cambridge University Press, 55–57.

[12]Turner, M. A., Fix, M., & Struyk, R. J. (1991). *Opportunities denied: Discrimination in hiring.* Washington, DC: Urban Institute.

[13]See Feagin & Sikes, *Living with racism.*

[14]U.S. Bureau of the Census. (1993). *Money income of households, families, and persons in the United States: 1992.* Washington, DC, xii; U.S. Bureau of the Census. (1993). *Poverty in the United States: 1992.* Washington, DC, xi; U.S. Bureau of the Census. (1990). *Household wealth and asset ownership: 1988.* Washington, DC, 8.

[15]Smith, L. (1961). *Killers of the dream* (Rev. ed.). New York: W. W. Norton, 68.

[16]Myrdal, *An American dilemma* (vol. 2). New York: McGraw-Hill; see also Banton, M. (1983). *Racial and ethnic competition.* Cambridge: Cambridge University Press; Katz, P. A., & Taylor, D. A. (1988). Introduction. In P. A. Katz & D. A. Taylor (Eds.), *Eliminating racism* (pp. 1–18). New York: Plenum.

[17]Pettigrew, T. (1975). Preface. In T. Pettigrew (Ed.), *Racial discrimination in the United States* (p. x). New York: Harper & Row.

[18]Feagin, J. R., & Feagin, C. B. (1978). *Discrimination American style: Institutional racism and sexism.* Englewood Cliffs, NJ: Prentice-Hall, 20–21.

[19]See Russell, P. (1983). *The global brain.* Boston: Houghton Mifflin, 115–118.

[20]See Kovel, J. (1984). *White racism: A psychohistory* (Rev. ed.). New York: Columbia University Press, xliv, 4.

[21]Smith, L. (1961). *Killers of the dream* (Rev. ed.). New York: W. W. Norton, 96.

[22]Smith, *op. cit.*, p. 27.

[23]Berkowitz, L. Some effects of thoughts on anti- and prosocial influences of media events. *Psychological Bulletin 9*, 410–427.

[24]Stearns, G. L. (Ed.). (1865). *The equality of all men before the law claimed and defended.* Boston, 38, quoted in Dykstra, R. R. (1993). *Bright radical star: Black freedom and white supremacy in the Hawkeye frontier.* Cambridge, MA: Harvard University Press, 269.

[25]Frankenberg, R. (1993). *White women, race matters.* Minneapolis, MN: University of Minnesota Press, 228–229.

[26]Frankenberg, R. *op. cit.*, p. 231.

◉ ◉ ◉

Questions

1. Define "white racism." How is white racism different from racism in general?

2. Why do Feagin and Vera claim that white racism is a theory of societal waste? To what degree is the waste associated solely with minority groups? In what way(s) is the waste more widespread and applicable to society as a whole?

3. How does a white person's sense of self or social identity contribute to white racism?

4. What role, if any, do structures of power play in a theory of white racism? Limiting power structures to the economy and the political arena, can you explain how these two structures have been used to contribute to white racism?

5. Young white Americans often argue that they have not owned slaves or discriminated against black people so they should not have to pay the price to solve racial discrimination. What would Feagin and Vera say to this?

6. What things must be done on the i
    racism? What must be done at the indivi
    willing to do?

mativity:

ons

orado

... are a woman, have you ever
asked a man to dance? If you are a man, have
... public or shaved your legs? How did others respond? This
article describes how, as part of a class assignment, students engaged in gender-
norm violations and how people responded to their behavior. The data they
gathered from this exercise illustrate how people generally interpret gender-
norm violations and how they sanction transgressors.

"here's a totally cute girl smoking a fucking cigar in my section," con-
fided a waitress to her manager in a restaurant in a university town.
The "totally cute girl" was case number 151 (1987), a sociology student
doing her gender norm violation project for her sex and gender in society
class. The waitress's statement is typical of reactions to women who "do
things members of your gender category don't usually do or don't do things
they usually do," as gender transgressions were defined for this assignment.
Reactions to male students' norm violations were similar. A young man who
proudly saved coupons for use at the grocery store (case number 185, 1986),
for example, reported that his mother wondered if he was "queer," encouraged him "to do something masculine," and refused to let him go to the grocery store with her. Others made comments such as, "You will sure make
some lucky girl a great househusband someday."

These and similar reports of 658 students' gender norm violations con-

"Gendered Heteronormativity: Empirical Illustrations in Everyday Life," by Joyce McCarl Nielsen,
Glenda Walden, and Charlotte A. Kunkel from *Sociological Quarterly*, Volume 41. Copyright © 2000
by the University of California Press. Reprinted with permission from the authors and the University
of California Press.

stitute the textual data for this article. These reports were generated in a rather unique manner, over a fifteen-year period from 1975–1990 as part of the authors' gender classes, in a university town whose population is primarily white, upper middle class, and young. Our interpretive analysis of students' written narratives of their experiences—what they did and their own and others' reactions—generated empirical findings relevant to radical feminist, queer, and cultural feminist theories on heterosexuality and gender.

In this article we argue that our students' gender transgressions evoked sanctionings that reflect the heterogendered and heteronormative expectations of institutionalized heterosexuality. The concepts "heterogender" and "heteronormativity" are two of many used in a growing body of primarily theoretical literature that problematizes heterosexuality (Adkins and Merchant 1996; Kitzinger, Wilkinson, and Perkins 1992; Maynard and Purvis 1995; Richardson 1996; Wilkinson and Kitzinger 1994). For example, scholars refer to heterosensibilities (Epstein and Steinberg 1995), heterosexual hegemony (e.g., Thompson 1992), heteropatriarchy (Ramazanoglu 1994), heterocentricity (Kitzinger et al. 1992), technologies of heterosexuality (Gavey 1993), and the heterosexual imaginary (Ingraham 1994). In various ways and to various degrees, these terms capture the taken-for-granted and simultaneously compulsory character of institutionalized heterosexuality. All are attempts to highlight an aspect of sexuality that is rarely stated (i.e., that heterosexuality is the default option) and to underscore its cultural dominance. This "studying up," as Michael Messner (1996) calls it (studying the more privileged side of a culture's constructed conceptual binaries) comes after years of focusing on the less privileged minority. This is a significant theoretical turn in feminist and queer theory and gender studies in general because of the connection between heterosexuality and gender inequality, a relation long-articulated by radical feminist theorists (MacKinnon 1989; Millett 1970; Rich 1980).

We develop and elaborate these themes by describing two gender-specific ways in which heterosexuality is managed and enforced. More specifically, we document how women transgressors in our study are primarily heterosexualized while the men are derogatorily labeled homosexual.

◉ Methods and Procedures

As feminist researcher-teachers (Maher and Tetreault 1994; Oakley 1981; Jayaratne and Stewart 1991), we considered the gender norm violation exercise both a research project and an opportunity for students to learn something about gender, power, and privilege. In this spirit, students functioned as both coresearchers and subjects in the data-generating process. They did brief fieldwork in natural settings (Lofland and Lofland 1995), collecting, recording, and reporting the data in textual narrative form (Ellis and Flaherty 1992). We then coded and analyzed the data and ongoingly shared aggregate results and interpretations with them, providing an opportunity for feedback and synthesis of their experiences with our aggregate preliminary analyses.

During the fieldwork phase student-researchers were required to have an accomplice to act as observer and record reactions that may be missed or hidden from those actively engaged in the action. The written reports were organized to include a narrative record of what action was taken, where and in what context it was done, the verbal and nonverbal reactions of others, and concluding thoughts or insights. These instructions produced data records that are more organized than field notes, but not as structured as recorded interviews. Each appears as an individually generated narrative about personal experience, guided by questions and implied standards of academic paper writing (Riessman 1993).

We use "narrative" to describe the data presented by the student-researchers, as it typically implies an underlying context, authority, and more formal, recognized format (Clandinin and Connelly 1994) than is usually found in student papers. They were not merely telling a "story" about their experience. Their texts were structured by temporality, authority of observation, academic standards, and the "writer's attempts to articulate some set of understandings about a particular situation, cultural form, or social process" (Denzin 1997, p. 235). These *original* texts, then, became "the site for new interpretive work," and our analysis constitutes a *new* "critical, interpretive text" (Denzin 1997, p. 235).

"Selection bias" on the part of student coresearchers is a potential limitation of the data. Although not a sampling issue in the strictest sense, this affects the generalizability of the findings (Neuman 1994). Students controlled what was observed, what was evaluated as significant, what was included in the narrative, and how that narrative was organized. They determined the length and degree of detail in the paper as well as coverage of direct quotes and qualifiers such as "It seemed that . . ." This, of course, is always the case with social research that relies on memories and honesty in constructing data sources. It is possible that sexual reactions were exaggerated (hence the check for fabrication—see below), that there were more reactions than observed and/or recorded, and that explicitly or overtly sexual reactions in particular were edited out as inappropriate for an academic paper. The latter case would only strengthen the assertions and inferences we make from these data.

After the papers were graded, students were asked to volunteer copies for this study. We were emphatic that this was not a course requirement, and no compensation was given for papers. Only six students over the years have declined this request. Each project was assigned a case number and names were removed from papers. Students were asked to indicate on the backside of the last page whether the fieldwork occurred as reported or was embellished or fabricated in any way. The small percentage of papers acknowledged by students as faked was not used in this study. In this respect, the narratives are as truthful and accurate as any interview or survey data and subject to the same risks of social desirability and nonresponse (or in this case, nonparticipation) bias (Neuman 1994).

The narrative data were transferred to coding sheets that separated and condensed pertinent information into the following format: (1) Who did what, when, and where? (e.g., "Woman smokes pipe at fraternity party" or "Man wears bright red nail polish to classes"), (2) reactions from others (e.g., "What a queer!" or "They looked at me funny"), (3) rationalizations, accounts, and explanations offered by student-researchers for why they're doing what they're doing while doing it (e.g., "I'm doing this for a class"), and finally (4) distinguishing features of each project recorded verbatim from the papers (e.g., "I felt hatred for those who stared [at me]").

The coded forms were read, reread, and analyzed by three independent researchers using the general method of grounded theory (Glaser and Strauss 1967). The coding process was not a one-time analysis. We revisited the narratives and reorganized and restructured the categories and themes many times, while maintaining and modifying concepts that emerged early in the process, and finally going to the literature for theoretical elaboration. With the number of cases available (N = 658) we easily reached theoretical saturation (Glaser and Strauss 1967). Three percent (N = 18) of the cases were uncodable, either because they were too poorly written to decipher, did not include enough information to categorize, or proved to be irrelevant to the conceptual scheme developed. These were not included in the analysis.

❧ Findings

"Norm violation category" (see list in Table 1) is based on the gender of the norm violator and the action taken (e.g., men carrying purses, men using women's bathrooms, women's knowledge of cars, women not doing housework, etc.). Table 1 is a complete list of project categories in order of frequency and whether the project was coded "explicitly sexual" or "unexplicitly sexual." The somewhat arbitrary nature of any categorization is revealed here. We realize that in everyday life, as well as in theoretical literature from Freud to feminism, there exists a continuum (rather than either/or categories) of perceived "sexualness." Every action, especially for women, according to Catherine A. MacKinnon (1989), is subject to sexualized interpretation. However, because early in the analysis we identified sexual interpretations of what appeared to be not inherently sexual actions (e.g., a man using grocery store coupons), we found it important to make this distinction. To clarify more precisely what we mean by "unexplicitly sexual," we argue that a man smoking a cigar may be considered "sexy" by some. Typically, though, his action is not interpreted as so overtly sexual that it would get him thrown out of public places, slapped by offended women, accused of perversions, or have his sexual preferences made explicit. Even Freud said, "Sometimes a cigar is just a cigar." On the other hand, a man buying a woman a drink in a bar is generally considered a polite sexual overture. We suggest that most women interpret such actions as indicating sexual interest. Therefore, we coded actions such as a woman buying a man a drink as "explicitly sexual." There were, of course, other actions in these projects that were more overtly sexual. There were also specific cases that prompted discussion and debate among the coders before settling on categorization precisely because they were not so easily coded as explicitly sexual or not. These controversial cases, however, do not detract from the main thesis of the article.

The above discussion refers to actions taken in the projects—what was done and how we coded it. In this section, we describe our coding of the students' and others' *interpretations* of the actions, using their exact words when possible and reporting only those unexplicitly sexual projects that were sexualized in one way or another. Sexualization took the form of assuming, questioning, and/or enforcing the norm violator's heterosexuality, sometimes simultaneously. Further, this reaction was always in terms of an assumed heterosexual/homosexual binary. The norm violator's sexual identity is problematized in that his/her taken-for-granted heterosexuality receives comment or is questioned. This occurred in two major ways, depending on whether the norm violator was male or female. For men, the most common reaction was to be labeled homosexual or potentially homosexual, as in the example of the young man saving coupons for grocery shopping. For women, the norm violator's ability to succeed within a taken-for-granted heterosexuality was challenged, as in the implied contradiction between being cute and

TABLE 1 *Gender Norm Violation Categories (No. in Parentheses)*

Women's Unexplicitly Sexual Norm Violations	Women's "Sexual" Norm Violations

Women's Unexplicitly Sexual Norm Violations

Buy/smoke cigar (24)
Buy/smoke pipe (19)
Buy/chew tobacco (19)
Cars: change tires, fix, buy parts, check under hood, test drive, talk knowledgeably about (18)
Enter/use men's bathroom (16)
Fight physically in public (13)
Open doors for men (10)
In "male" occupations (e.g., pilot, lawyer, army combat, geologist, carpenter, bouncer, construction) (10)
Do not do routine housework (9)
Ask man out, pay for date (9)
Be verbally loud and aggressive (watching sports, greeting) (8)
Go shirtless in sports context (7)
Buy/try on men's suits, ties (5)
Spit in public (4)
Wear mustache (4)
Talk about menstruation (3)
Work out in male weight room (3)
Buy, rent, ask about construction products (3)
Wear men's cologne (3)
Buy jock strap (3)
Walk alone, go out at night alone (3)
Wear football uniform (2)
Wear Rambo outfit, army fatigues (2)
Send man flowers (2)
Eat a lot in public (2)
Play poker with "boys" (2)
Do not shave legs, underarms (2)
Wear men's wallets, money clip (2)
Burp, belch, pass gas in public (2)
Plays dumb about laundry (1)
Gives seat to men (1)
Seats men, holds coats (1)
Beat man at pool (1)
Play basketball with men (1)
Challenge man at tennis, racquetball (1)
Do martial arts (1)
Ride skateboard (1)
Adjust and spit before batting (1)
Sit with legs apart (1)
Wear and display tattoo (1)
Appear bald (1)
Wear skullcap to synagogue (1)
Dress as priest (1)
Appear androgynous (1)
Urinate outside on road (1)
Don't smile as receptionist (1)
Go to all male country club (1)
Go hunting with men (1)
Go to fraternity rush (1)
Be on all-male church committee (1)

Women's "Sexual" Norm Violations

Ask men to dance, buy men drinks, try to pick up men, in bars (38)
Violate heterosexual norm—date, dance with, be affectionate toward women, go to gay bars (22)
Go to strip/topless bar (19)
Catcall, wink, or whistle at, watch, rate men's bodies in public (18)
Go to porn store (17)
Buy condoms (13)
Touch, pinch, pat men (11)
Buy man engagement ring (5)
Read *Playgirl* (4)
Ask men to pose nude (4)
Make obscene phone calls (3)
Brag, talk about sex (2)
Read, use pornography (2)
Propose marriage (2)
Put ad in paper for man (1)
Scratch crotch (1)
Tell dirty jokes (1)

Men's Unexplicitly Sexual Norm Violations

Try on, wear, buy women's clothing and/or women's shoes in public (28)
Wear makeup, lipstick, and/or have makeover (22)

115

Shave body hair, color or curl hair, wear flower in hair (8)

Wear, put on fingernails, fingernail polish, have manicure (23)

Wear earrings[a] (9)

Do or help with housework, grocery shopping, be househusband (9)

Apply for or do "women's" occupation—day care, baby sit, rape counselor (8)

Do needlepoint, crochet, knit in public (7)

Cry in public (5)

Carry purse (5)

Enter, use women's restroom (3)

Show interest in bridal registry (2)

Buy sanitary napkins (2)

Ask woman to pay for dinner (2)

Talk as though feminist (2)

Wear pink shirts for a week (1)

Have pedicure (1)

Let woman beat him in track (1)

Show an interest in fashion (1)

Primp hair (1)

Wear apron and hairnet (1)

Use limp handshake (1)

Throw Tupperware party (1)

Dance woman's part of square dance (1)

Play bridesmaid during wedding rehearsal (1)

Read romance novels (1)

Men's "Sexual" Norm Violations

Violate heterosexual norm—dance with, be affectionate with men, go to gay bars (21)

Wear, try on women's underwear, halter top, nightgown, bathing suit (12)

Perform in male beauty pageant (1)

[a]See note 1 in text regarding men wearing earrings.

smoking a cigar, or as in cases where women are defined as not "kissable" or not "datable" because they are chewing tobacco (case number 362, 1983) or smoking a pipe (case number 172, 1986), respectively. Thus, sexualization, was divided into three categories: homophobic disclaimers, homosexualization, and heterosexualization. Heterosexualization, in turn, is further specified along a continuum from indirect to overt to hyperheterosexualization. We refer collectively to these three categories as heterogender (i.e., defining women and men in terms of their heterosexual relationship potential such as whether one is kissable, datable, or would be a good partner).

Bisexual interpretations of these projects are noteworthy for their absence. Only one paper in the 658 generated over the fifteen-year period contained a statement about bisexuality: a reference to "crazy bisexual girls" who used men's bathrooms. Although bisexuality as a possible explanation for these projects seems plausible, it is apparently outside students' and others' culturally and historically specific interpretive paradigms. This is an important finding in itself and points to an integral part of the heterosexualization process, that of making alternatives invisible.

We present the findings according to how different actions were interpreted rather than by categories of what the students did. This emphasizes the fact that a wide variety of unexplicitly sexual projects led to a few similarly patterned reactions. Indeed, reactions, responses, and interpretations were more easily categorized than were project actions. Note the number of categories in Table 1 with few or only one case, indicating a wide variety of projects created and enacted by the student-researchers. Yet the dominant reactions are in terms of heterogender even when the activities did not involve explicitly sexual interactions or traditionally recognized sexual indicators. Even very unique projects, such as the man who hosted a Tupperware party and women who wore moustaches, received responses little different than more routine or common projects, such as men wearing women's clothing and women "hitting" on men. These patterns underscore the importance of the fact that a gender transgression, rather than its exact nature or content, activates heteronormative prescriptions.

Further, we discovered that with the possible exception of men wearing earrings (and now women smoking cigars[1]), the year of the project was not related to either what was done or how it was interpreted by students and others. The year of each project is reported after the case number to demonstrate our sensitivity to time contexts and to give an indication of the lack of pattern over time.

The single most dominant theme in the papers was that of heterogender. Explicitly sexual norm violations (e.g., same-sex dancing, embracing, and holding hands; women catcalling men and rating their bodies) elicited sexual interpretations more often than did unexplicitly sexual ones, as might be expected. More interesting, though, is the relatively large number of unexplicitly sexual projects that elicited heterogendered interpretations. These are further elaborated below.

◉ Heterogender

Homophobic Disclaimers by Gender Norm Violators

A noticeable number of women and men students began their reports by proclaiming their heterosexuality, apparently in an attempt to counter the possibility that we (the *only* readers of their papers) or others knowledgeable about the project might think they were gay. This occurred in many projects of violating explicitly heterosexual norms and was often accompanied by denouncing homosexuality and/or expressing fear about being seen as homosexual. However, students also tried to manage their self-presentations in sexual terms while doing less explicitly sexual gender norm violations. The man who hosted a Tupperware party (case number 532, 1990), for

117

example, advised his male guests as they were arriving, "Just keep in the back of your mind, no matter what goes on tonight, I am not gay." Another man who painted his fingernails "cherry red" (case number 005, 1986) told three different bystanders that it was for a class and noticed that "they were relieved that I was not gay or something." Another man (case number 135, 1990) who used a "limp fish" handshake in three different settings for his project reported that he was so worried about being thought gay that he "talked solely about women [in order] to assure John he was hetero—not gay." This same student entitled his paper "Gay or Not Gay?" These examples illustrate nicely the employment of a homo/hetero binary and self-regulation and management on the part of norm violators as they anticipated questions about and affirmed their heterosexuality. They avoided and corrected potential misperceptions about their heterosexuality, even to strangers.

❧ Homosexual Labeling

Homosexual labeling refers to culturally defined and derogatory labels for gays and lesbians such as "fag" and "dyke." When spoken by others, we called it "external" homophobia; when spoken by the norm violators themselves, we called it "internal" homophobia. We recognize that these terms have been reclaimed and resignified within some homosexual communities and could be used in positive and gay- and lesbian-affirming ways. Our sense, though, is that this was not the purpose of their use here. As the examples illustrate, the labels were used to mark and set apart what was seen as gender inappropriate behavior and to define it as sexually deviant.

The men doing these projects were blatantly, overtly, and derogatorily labeled homosexual. Reactions to them took the form of making fun of and joking about the norm violator by implying that he appeared or acted "like a woman" and/or "gay" at the same time.

The students articulated common associations between certain (unexplicitly sexual) acts and being gay. For example, one young man wrote:

> I viewed the earring as a symbol of freedom, and in its other context, as a symbol of being feminine and perverted—a trademark of homosexuals, (case number 332, 1979; see note 1 regarding the changing cultural meaning of men wearing earrings).

Similarly, a man who visited a makeup counter (case number 021, 1981) reflected: "Man's use of makeup [is an] act of vanity or worse, leading towards homosexuality."

The same theme of confounding unexplicitly sexual but "feminine" or women-related acts with homosexuality is illustrated in several cases of norm violations that involved men buying feminine articles of clothing or personal hygiene. In two cases, bystanders and beauty sales clerks said, "He didn't look gay," and "I didn't know he was gay until he opened his mouth" (case numbers 046, 1983 and 352, 1988, respectively). When one man confessed that his manicure was a school project (case number 586, 1977), the manicurist responded, "I thought so, because you don't look gay." The same man reported that his friends jokingly called him a "fag." A man who wore earrings for his project (case number 332, 1979) reported that his girlfriend asked him to stop wearing them because they made him "look gay."

Reactions to a man who wore a flower in his hair (case number 554, 1979) were, "Gee, you look thweet [sic] today" and "We gotta sweet fella here." A man who wore a skirt around campus and in a nearby city generated the comment, "What a fag!" (case number 001, 1988). Two men who wore dresses to a local bar were told, "Fairies aren't allowed in here" (case number 324, 1979). Another two men who wore dresses (case number 111, 1981) reported being taunted, "Look at the fuckin' queers!" and "Hey, fag, how about a dance?" Again, unexplicitly sexual actions were sexualized.

Female gender transgressors were similarly but less frequently subjected to homophobia. For example, a woman who staged a fight with a man in a bar and punched him was described by a stranger as "a little dyke-y" (case number 767, 1982). And a woman and man who did a dating role reversal at a party and in a bar (case number 234, 1990) were called "dyke, bitch" and "faggot," respectively.

Though less often labeled gay in a derogatory way by others (external homophobia), women students expressed concern about being thought gay (internal homophobia). To illustrate the degree of this concern and the theme of homophobia that was present in a wide variety of projects, we list the following: Women expressed concern about being thought of as gay when they wore men's cologne (case number 309, 1987), worked out in an all-male weight room (case number 704, 1978), did not shave their legs or underarms (case numbers 152, 1987 and 483, 1988), tried on men's suits (case number 754, 1976), wore men's suits and ties to a sorority dinner (case number 415, 1990), visited a bar alone (case number 133, 1990), smoked a pipe (case number 286, 1978), and bought and smoked a cigar (case number 494, 1986). The case of a woman who asked a male coworker to dinner (case number 034, 1979) and worried that he would think she was a lesbian is particularly illustrative because it highlights the potential of *any* act being labeled homosexual. A woman asking a man out could be considered evidence of her heterosexuality rather than homosexuality, yet because the woman is doing the asking, she worried that he might think she was gay!

Case number 770 (1975), a woman who wore a moustache, illustrates both internal homophobia and heterosexualization. She reported "[I] had to fight myself not to put on makeup—which I usually don't wear in the first place (desire to affirm my sexual identity?)," and she was greeted with the words, "How about a morning kiss? No, I changed my mind."

❧ ✋eterosexualization

For women, compulsory heterosexuality was imposed through heterosexualization that ranged from indirect to overt to hyperheterosexualization. Women were judged and evaluated primarily in terms of the action's effect on their attractiveness to men. There were no cases of men students being heterosexualized (i.e., evaluated in terms of their attractiveness to women).

✐ndirect ✋eterosexualization

Indirect heterosexualization refers to attractiveness and availability on the part of women to men (e.g., whether a woman is pretty, cute, or would be nice to kiss). For example, a woman who inquired about wood at a building supply store (case number 095, 1983) was described by a man as "one of the prettiest carpenters he'd ever seen." And two women who staged a fight (case number 682) were asked, "Is this any way for two pretty young girls to behave?" Here, women were given advice in heterosexual terms. A woman who smoked a cigar in front of her family and friends (case number 446, 1977), for example, was advised by her mother to "not do it in front of men."

In another example, a man responded to a woman chewing tobacco (case number 649, 1990), "A girl has never asked me for a chew before. And I never expected she would be cute when she did." The point of being described as cute was not lost on the norm violator. She wrote "His . . . comment on my being cute really upset me . . . I interpreted . . . that a woman can only be a real woman when she . . . keeps . . . her femininity." Another woman who smoked a cigar at a fraternity party (case number 400, 1987) noted that "the cigar prevented men from approaching her to hit on her."

Overt Heterosexualization

Other projects generated even more explicit references to women's sexual availability and sexual innuendo. For example, a female coal miner (case number 679, 1979) was told, "You should be posing in the centerfold of *Playboy* instead of working in a mine." Another woman who was wearing a toolbelt and steel toe boots (case number 523, 1988) reported she felt "hustled" when a man asked suggestively, "Do you really know how to use all these tools?" Although these women were actually doing their (nonsexual) jobs, they were defined or addressed in heterosexual terms.

The following examples of the importance of women's being attractive in order to maintain socially recognized relationships with men illustrate another aspect of heteronormativity. In case number 172 (1986), a woman smoked a pipe in front of her husband's seminar group. One comment was, "It's a good thing she's married because she probably wouldn't get any dates." Two women who chewed tobacco and smoked cigars in a university town setting (case number 517, 1988) reported an onlooker saying "I would never date someone that [sic] smokes cigars." In case number 182 (1986) a woman who wore a mustache to a university town bar to meet a blind date was described as one who will "never find a husband."

Case number 141 (1990) illustrates more overt heterosexualization. A woman mechanic who worked on cars both at home and in a garage reported that one man said, "Thank you," leered at her, and "stroked my hand suggestively." Men often responded to women's gender transgressions with enthusiastic sexual interest. For example, one man's reactions to a woman asking him to dance (case number 287, 1978) said, "God bless, it's a first. Let's go to my car." The same eagerness showed up in unexplicitly sexual projects. For example, two women who applied for typically "male" jobs (case number 735, 1977) were told, "You don't look much like mechanics, but why don't we discuss it over drinks." Though dismissed as mechanics, they were seen as potential dates.

Even actions (by women) that violated standards of personal privacy in gendered space (Goffman 1977)—for example, women entering men's bathrooms—elicited sexual remarks. Comments such as "You don't have to leave yet, baby," "Do you want to hold my hand?" (case number 029, 1986), and "Want to give me a quickie while you're here?" (case number 418, 1990) were reported.

A woman who sent flowers to a man (case number 471, 1981) wrote (to justify her norm violation?), "The girl has just as much right to fuck around as a guy does," as though sending flowers meant a sexual encounter.

Hyperheterosexualization: Attributed Promiscuity

Finally, a frequent response to women's projects was attribution of heightened or hyperheterosexual activity. The students' sexual appetites or tastes were questioned and/or labeled "promiscuous" by others and sometimes by themselves. A woman who sat with her legs apart at school, a shopping mall, and a wedding (case number 186, 1986), for example, reflected: "People seemed to interpret my position as promiscuous instead of masculine." This example nicely captures the tendency to interpret women's behavior in heterosexual terms, since her project was simply to imitate male body language. Another woman's male friends told her that her sending a man a flower (case number 218, 1986) was just a subtle way of letting him know that she wanted to sleep with him. Finally, when a woman decided to go hunting with her husband and his friends (case number 629, 1977), she reported: "One girl called me on the phone, insinuating that I was some sort of sex maniac." She added, "Most of the wives jumped to the conclusion that I was after their husbands."

These examples illustrate that when women do things they don't usually do, they are often interpreted as sexually aggressive and heterosexually promiscuous, even when there is no overt or explicit sexual message. In short, heterosexuality is implied through reference to women's attractiveness to men, through sexual innuendo, and through emphasizing sexuality in male-female relationships. These patterns illustrate how "compulsory" heterosexuality thoroughly colonizes women's everyday lives such that even overt acts of gender and sexual rebellion are dismissed or trivialized.

❧ Discussion

Our findings may be succinctly summarized. The routinely unquestioned heteronormative expectations and proscriptions that exist as background context in contemporary U.S. culture emerge when traditional normative gender boundaries are crossed. Further, heteronormativity itself is gendered via the homosexualization of disruptive men and the heterosexualization of disruptive women. This work contributes in several ways to our understanding of institutionalized heterosexuality and its operation in everyday life.

First, although much is made of the distinction between institutionalized and lived or experienced heterosexuality (e.g., Jackson 1996), our findings underscore the extent to which heteronormative expectations intrude into everyday lived experience. It is not that the unacknowledged privileges of everyday life associated with being heterosexual or the disadvantages of being homosexual have never been spelled out in the literature. Indeed, they have. However, our illustrations of individuals coming face to face with an explicitly articulated discourse of institutionalized heterosexuality, precisely because they crossed a gender boundary, are rather dramatic. They expose the interconnected nature of social structure and individual experience, as well as the intricate relation between gender and sexuality.

Further, even though we talk about institutionalized heterosexuality as taken for granted and assumed, our findings show the extent to which heterosexuality requires active maintenance. It appears to be vigorously enforced (both internally and externally) through a combination of stigmatizing and rendering invisible any alternatives to it. At the same time, we see the everyday conflation of gender and sexuality. For men, a gender violation threatens loss of masculine heterosexual privilege; for women, it generates evaluations of their sexual availability and desirability to men. Knowing how and of what gender and institutionalized heterosexuality are socially constructed can guide our dismantling of them.

While these themes are discussed in the literature, it is useful to flesh them out with relatively rich, systematic data. Moreover, our illustrations fill an empirical void. Both Rosemary Pringle (1992) and Steven Seidman (1996) point out that a demonstration of heteronormativity in lived experience has been missing in social research and theory, even though its presence in cultural images and texts is relatively well analyzed. The value of empirical inquiry is even better illustrated in cases where hypotheses from the literature are controversial or contradicted by findings. A case in point is Allan Hunter's (1992) speculation that the conceptual bond between masculinity and heterosexuality for males is not as strong as that between femininity and heterosexuality for females. Our data suggest that the difference is in qualitative content rather than degree. In any case, it is unusual to bring together in one article a discussion of how compulsory heterosexuality operates differently for women *and* men. Although gender scholars in a variety of disciplines recognize constitutive connections between heterosexual masculinity and homophobia (Connell 1992; Herek 1986; Lehne [1980] 1998) and between heterosexual femininity and gender inequality, these themes are more often separated into different articles and texts.

We do not measure or examine gender inequality directly, but our findings are relevant to theoretical work that relates sexuality and gender inequality. A central premise of early radical feminist thought is that "heterosexuality is the linchpin of gender inequality" (MacKinnon 1989, p. 113). Adrienne Rich (1980) articulated its institutionalized character with the phrase "compulsory heterosexuality." Many gender scholars routinely accept that the gender system is predicated on the control of women's sexuality (Renzetti and Curran 1999; Lorber 1994), even though other sites of women's subordination (such as the appropriation of women's labor) are also acknowledged. Queer theorists (Fuss 1991; Richardson 1996; Rubin 1984; Warner 1993) and feminist cultural theorists (e.g., Butler 1991) have further developed the idea that institutionalized heterosexuality is at the intersection of the gender and sexuality systems. Their point is that heterogender rather than gender per se is the basis of inequality (Ingraham 1994). Our findings are consistent with this approach to gender stratification. Further, the examples presented here suggest that a key component of maintaining gender inequality and heterosexual privilege is upholding and highlighting differences—differences in appearance and action between women and men. It is primarily when women do "male" things and vice versa that questions about sexuality come into play. Although many writers, queer theorists in particular, emphasize that it is not differences per se but their evaluation and cultural meanings that are key to social inequality, our findings stress the critical role of upholding differences in maintaining heterogender. Thus, "sameness" may be more important for equality than previously thought.

This necessarily brief discussion of the implications of our findings shows that their value is in their potential for further refinement and elaboration of existing gender theories. At a more practical level, a more thorough and complete understanding of the (hetero) sex/gender system—its points of vulnerability as well as its routine operation—will lead to more opportunities for transcending heterogender itself.

ℰndnote

[1]Men wearing earrings is the only action whose cultural meaning has changed during the data collection period (1975–1990). In the geographical area in which most projects were done, men wearing one or two earrings in the 1970s was commonly interpreted as a marker for homosexuality. In the 1980s, it was common for straight men to wear an earring in the left ear. In the 1990s, anything goes—

there are no clear-cut markers, though it is still unusual for straight men to wear earrings in both ears. Women smoking cigars was a viable gender norm violation throughout the 1975–1990 period. Now, in the 1990s, women smoking cigars has become fashionable—for some perhaps even sexual. Both men wearing earrings and women smoking cigars are coded as nonsexual projects in Table 1.

References

Adkins, Lisa, and Vicki Merchant, eds. 1996. *Sexualizing the Social: Power and the Organization of Sexuality.* New York: St. Martin's Press.

Butler, Judith. 1990. *Gender Trouble: Feminism and the Subversion of Identity.* New York: Routledge.

———. 1991. "Imitation and Gender Insubordination." Pp. 13–31 in *Inside/Out,* edited by Diana Fuss. New York: Routledge.

———. 1993. *Bodies that Matter: On the Discursive Limits of Sex.* New York: Routledge.

Clandinin, D. Jean, and F. Michael Connelly. 1994. "Personal Experience Methods." Pp. 413–427 in *Handbook of Qualitative Research,* edited by Norman K. Denzin and Yvonna S. Lincoln. Thousand Oaks, CA: Sage.

Connell, R. W. 1992. "A Very Straight Gay: Masculinity, Homosexual Experience, and the Dynamics of Gender." *American Sociological Review* 57:735–751.

Denzin, Norman K. 1997. *Interpretive Ethnography: Ethnographic Practices for the 21st Century.* Thousand Oaks, CA: Sage.

Ellis, Carolyn, and Michael G. Flaherty. 1992. "An Agenda for the Interpretation of Lived Experience." Pp. 1–13 in *Investigating Subjectivity: Research on Lived Experience,* edited by Carolyn Ellis and Michael G. Flaherty. Newbury Park, CA: Sage.

Epstein, Debbie, and Deborah Lynn Steinberg. 1995. "Twelve Steps to Heterosexuality? Commonsensibilities on the Oprah Winfrey Show." *Feminism and Psychology* 5:275–280.

Frankenberg, Ruth. 1993. *White Women, Race Matters: The Social Construction of Whiteness.* Minneapolis: University of Minnesota Press.

Fuss, Diana. 1991. *Inside/Out: Lesbian Theories, Gay Theories.* New York: Routledge.

Gavey, Nicola. 1993. "Technologies and Effects of Heterosexual Coercion." Pp. 93–119 in *Heterosexuality: A Feminism and Psychology Reader,* edited by Sue Wilkinson and Celia Kitzinger. London: Sage.

Gilfoyle, Jackie, Jonathan Wilson, and Brown. 1993. "Sex, Organs and Audiotape: A Discourse Analytic Approach to Talking About Heterosexual Sex and Relationships." Pp. 181–202 in *Heterosexuality: A Feminism and Psychology Reader,* edited by Sue Wilkinson and Celia Kitzinger. Newbury Park, CA: Sage.

Glaser, Barney G., and Anselm L. Strauss. 1967. *The Discovery of Grounded Theory.* New York: Aldine de Gruyter.

Goffman, Erving. 1977. "The Arrangement between the Sexes." *Theory and Society* 4:301–331.

Herek, Gregory M. 1986. "On Heterosexual Masculinity: Some Psychical Consequences of the Social Construction of Gender and Sexuality." *American Behavioral Scientist* 29:563–577.

Hunter, Allan. 1992. "Same Door, Different Closet: A Heterosexual Sissy's Coming-out Party." *Feminism and Psychology* 2:327–385.

Ingraham, Chrys. 1994. "The Heterosexual Imaginary: Feminist Sociology and Theories of Gender." *Sociological Theory* 12:203–219.

Jackson, Stevi. 1996. "Heterosexuality and Feminist Theory." Pp. 21–38 in *Theorising Heterosexuality: Telling It Straight,* edited by Diane Richardson. Buckingham, UK: Open University Press.

Jayaratne, Toby Epstein, and Abigail Stewart. 1991. "Quantitative and Qualitative Methods in the Social Sciences: Current Feminist Issues and Practical Strategies." Pp. 85–106 in *Beyond Methodology: Feminist Scholarship as Lived Research,* edited by Mary Margaret Fonow and Judith Cook. Bloomington: Indiana University Press.

Kitzinger, Celia, Sue Wilkinson, and Rachel Perkins. 1992. "Editorial Introduction: Theorizing Heterosexuality." *Feminism and Psychology* 2:293–324.

Lehne, Gregory K. [1980]1998. "Homophobia among Men: Supporting and Defining the Male Role." Pp. 237–253 in *Men's Lives,* 4th ed. edited by Michael S. Kimmel and Michael A. Messner. Boston: Allyn and Bacon.

Lofland, John, and Lyn H. Lofland. 1995. *Analyzing Social Settings: A Guide to Qualitative Observation and Analysis.* Belmont, CA: Wadsworth.

Lorber, Judith. 1994. *Paradoxes of Gender.* New Haven, CT: Yale University Press.

MacKinnon, Catherine A. 1989. *Toward a Feminist Theory of the State.* Cambridge, MA: Harvard University Press.

Maher, Frances A., and Mary Kay Thompson Tetreault. 1994. *The Feminist Classroom.* New York: Basic Books.

Maynard, Mary, and June Purvis. 1995. *(Hetero)sexual Politics.* London: Taylor and Francis.

Messner, Michael. 1996. "Studying Up on Sex." *Sociology of Sport Journal* 6(13):221–237.

Millett, Kate. 1970. *Sexual Politics.* Garden City, NY: Doubleday.

Neuman, W. Lawrence. 1994. *Social Research Methods: Qualitative and Quantitative Approaches,* 2nd ed. Boston: Allyn and Bacon.

Nielsen, Joyce McCarl. 1990. *Sex and Gender in Society: Perspectives on Stratification,* 2nd ed. Prospect Heights, IL: Waveland Press.

Oakley, Anne. 1981. "Interviewing Women: A Contradiction in Terms." Pp. 30–61 in *Doing Feminist Research,* edited by Helen Roberts. London: Routledge and Kegan Paul.

Pringle, Rosemary. 1992. "Absolute Sex? Unpacking the Sexuality/Gender Relationship." Pp. 76–101 in *Rethinking Sex: Social Theory and Sexuality Research,* edited by R. W. Connell and G. W. Dowsett. Philadelphia, PA: Temple University Press.

Ramazanoglu, Caroline. 1994. "Theorizing Heterosexuality: A Response to Wendy Hollway." *Feminism and Psychology* 4:320–321.

Renzetti, Claire M., and Daniel J. Curran. [1989]1999. *Women, Men, and Society,* 4th ed. Boston: Allyn and Bacon.

Rich, Adrianne. 1980. "Compulsory Heterosexuality and Lesbian Existence." *Signs: Journal of Women in Culture and Society* 5:631–660.

Richardson, Diane. 1996. "Heterosexuality and Social Theory." Pp. 1–20 in *Theorising Heterosexuality: Telling it Straight,* edited by Diane Richardson. Buckingham: Open University Press.

Riessman, Catherine Kohler. 1993. *Narrative Analysis.* Newbury Park, CA: Sage.

Rubin, Gayle. 1984. "Thinking Sex: Notes for a Radical Theory of the Politics of Sexuality." Pp. 267–319 in *Pleasure and Danger: Exploring Female Sexuality,* edited by Carole S. Vance. Boston: Routledge and Kegan Paul.

Sedgwick, Eve Kosofsky. 1991. *Epistemology of the Closet.* Berkeley: University of California Press.

Seidman, Steven, ed. 1996. *Queer Theory/Sociology.* Cambridge, MA: Blackwell.

Thompson, Denise. 1992. "Against the Dividing of Women: Lesbian Feminism and Heterosexuality." *Feminism and Psychology* 2:387–398.

Warner, Michael. 1993. "Introduction." Pp. vii–xxxi in *Fear of a Queer Planet,* edited by Michael Warner. Minneapolis: University of Minnesota Press.

Wilkinson, Sue, and Celia Kitzinger. 1994. *Journal of Gender Studies* 3(3):307–316.

◉ ◉ ◉

Questions

1. How did the researchers gather data for this qualitative study? Can you think of other ways in which they could have learned about how people interpret gender-norm violations?

2. Define and illustrate what the authors mean by "heteronormativity." How can it be seen as a social problem?

3. Describe the differences between how women and men were evaluated for violating gender norms. Why do you think people responded so differently to the men who violated gender norms than they did to the women?

4. Briefly describe something you have done in the past that violated a gender norm. How did people respond to your infraction? Do you still engage in this behavior? Why, or why not?

5. List five things that you think qualify as gender-norm violations for women, and then for men. Bring your lists to class and combine them with the other students' lists. How do the items on the combined lists compare to those in Table 1? What does this suggest about what constitutes deviant behavior?

Millions for Viagra, Pennies for Diseases of the Poor

KEN SILVERSTEIN

Why are pharmaceutical companies willing to invest millions of dollars on drugs that reduce wrinkles or that eliminate our pets' anxiety—and not on drugs that would eradicate life-threatening illness afflicting Third World populations? The answer is related to how global economic stratification affects the availability of health care—those who can pay get what they need and want from the medical institution, and those who can't may not.

Put another way, the lure of high profits encourages pharmaceutical companies to place a priority on developing "lifestyle" drugs like Viagra, Rogaine, or even antidepressants for pets over developing drugs for infectious diseases such as malaria or river blindness. And, as Ken Silverstein argues, until it is profitable for them to do so, pharmaceutical companies are unlikely to change their priorities to research, develop, and introduce affordable drugs to disadvantaged populations.

*A*lmost three times as many people, most of them in tropical countries of the Third World, die of preventable, curable diseases as die of AIDS. Malaria, tuberculosis, acute lower-respiratory infections—in 1998, these claimed 6.1 million lives. People died because the drugs to treat those illnesses are nonexistent or are no longer effective. They died because it doesn't pay to keep them alive.

Only 1 percent of all new medicines brought to market by multinational pharmaceutical companies between 1975 and 1997 were designed specifically to treat tropical diseases plaguing the Third World. In numbers, that means thirteen out of 1,223 medications. Only four of those thirteen resulted from research by the industry that was designed specifically to combat tropical ailments. The others, according to a study by the French group Doctors

Without Borders, were either updated versions of existing drugs, products of military research, accidental discoveries made during veterinary research or, in one case, a medical breakthrough in China.

Certainly, the majority of the other 1,210 new drugs help relieve suffering and prevent premature death, but some of the hottest preparations, the ones that, as the *New York Times* put it, drug companies "can't seem to roll . . . out fast enough," have absolutely nothing to do with matters of life and death. They are what have come to be called lifestyle drugs—remedies that may one day free the world from the scourge of toenail fungus, obesity, baldness, face wrinkles and impotence. The market for each drug is worth billions of dollars a year and is one of the fastest-growing product lines in the industry.

The drug industry's calculus in apportioning its resources is cold-blooded, but there's no disputing that one old, fat, bald, fungus-ridden rich man who can't get it up counts for more than half a billion people who are vulnerable to malaria but too poor to buy the remedies they need.

Western interest in tropical diseases was historically linked to colonization and war, specifically the desire to protect settlers and soldiers. Yellow fever became a target of biomedical research only after it began interfering with European attempts to control parts of Africa. "So obvious was this deterrence . . . that it was celebrated in song and verse by people from Sudan to Senegal," Laurie Garrett recounts in her extraordinary book *The Coming Plague*. "Well into the 1980s schoolchildren in Ibo areas of Nigeria still sang the praises of mosquitoes and the diseases they gave to French and British colonialists."

US military researchers have discovered virtually all important malaria drugs. Chloroquine was synthesized in 1941 after quinine, until then the primary drug to treat the disease, became scarce following Japan's occupation of Indonesia. The discovery of Mefloquine, the next advance, came about during the Vietnam War, in which malaria was second only to combat wounds in sending US troops to the hospital. With the end of a ground-based US military strategy came the end of innovation in malaria medicine.

The Pharmaceutical Research and Manufacturers of America (PhRMA) claimed in newspaper ads early this year that its goal is to "set every last disease on the path to extinction." Jeff Trewhitt, a PhRMA spokesman, says US drug companies will spend $24 billion on research this year and that a number of firms are looking for cures for tropical diseases. Some companies also provide existing drugs free to poor countries, he says. "Our members are involved. There's not an absolute void."

The void is certainly at hand. Neither PhRMA nor individual firms will reveal how much money the companies spend on any given disease—that's proprietary information, they say—but on malaria alone, a recent survey of the twenty-four biggest drug companies found that not a single one maintains an in-house research program, and only two expressed even minimal interest in primary research on the disease. "The pipeline of available drugs is almost empty," says Dyann Wirth of the Harvard School of Public Health, who conducted the study. "It takes five to ten years to develop a new drug, so we could soon face [a strain of] malaria resistant to every drug in the world." A 1996 study presented in *Cahiers Santé,* a French scientific journal, found that of forty-one important medicines used to treat major tropical diseases, none were discovered in the nineties and all but six were discovered before 1985.

Contributing to this trend is the wave of mergers that has swept the industry over the past decade. Merck alone now controls almost 10 percent of the world market. "The bigger they grow, the more they decide that their research should be focused on the most profitable diseases and conditions," one industry watcher says. "The only thing the companies think about on a daily basis is the price of their stocks; and announcing that you've discovered a drug [for a tropical disease] won't do much for your share price."

That comment came from a public health advocate, but it's essentially seconded by industry. "A corporation with stockholders can't stoke up a laboratory that will focus on Third World diseases, because it will go broke," says Roy Vagelos, the former head of Merck. "That's a social problem, and industry shouldn't be expected to solve it."

Drug companies, however, are hardly struggling to beat back the wolves of bankruptcy. The pharmaceutical sector racks up the largest legal profits of any industry, and it is expected to grow by an average of 16 to 18 percent over the next four years, about three times more than the average for the Fortune 500. Profits are especially high in the United States, which alone among First World nations does not control drug prices. As a result, prices here are about twice as high as they are in the European Union and nearly four times higher than in Japan.

"It's obvious that some of the industry's surplus profits could be going into research for tropical diseases," says a retired drug company executive, who wishes to remain anonymous. "Instead, it's going to stockholders." Also to promotion: In 1998, the industry unbuckled $10.8 billion on advertising.

And to politics: In 1997, American drug companies spent $74.8 million to lobby the federal government, more than any other industry; last year they spent nearly $12 million on campaign contributions.

Just forty-five years ago, the discovery of new drugs and pesticides led the World Health Organization (WHO) to predict that malaria would soon be eradicated. By 1959, Garrett writes in *The Coming Plague,* the Harvard School of Public Health was so certain that the disease was passé that its curriculum didn't offer a single course on the subject.

Resistance to existing medicines—along with cutbacks in healthcare budgets, civil war and the breakdown of the state—has led to a revival of malaria in Africa, Latin America, Southeast Asia and, most recently, Armenia and Tajikistan. The WHO describes the disease as a leading cause of global suffering and says that by "undermining the health and capacity to work of hundreds of millions of people, it is closely linked to poverty and contributes significantly to stunting social and economic development."

Total global expenditures for malaria research in 1993, including government programs, came to $84 million. That's paltry when you consider that one B-2 bomber costs $2 billion, the equivalent of what, at current levels, will be spent on all malaria research over twenty years. In that period, some 40 million Africans alone will die from the disease. In the United States, the Pentagon budgets $9 million per year for malaria programs, about one-fifth the amount it set aside this year to supply the troops with Viagra. For the drug companies, the meager purchasing power of malaria's victims leaves the disease off the radar screen. As Neil Sweig, an industry analyst at Southeast Research Partners, puts it wearily, "It's not worth the effort or the while of the large pharmaceutical companies to get involved in enormously expensive research to conquer the Anopheles mosquito."

The same companies that are indifferent to malaria are enormously troubled by the plight of dysfunctional First World pets. John Keeling, a spokesman for the Washington, DC–based Animal Health Institute, says the "companion animal" drug market is exploding, with US sales for 1998 estimated at about $1 billion. On January 5, the FDA approved the use of Clomicalm, produced by Novartis, to treat dogs that suffer from separation anxiety (warning signs: barking or whining, "excessive greeting" and chewing on furniture). "At Last, Hope for Millions of Suffering Canines Worldwide," reads the company's press release announcing the drug's rollout. "I can't emphasize enough how dogs are suffering and that their behavior is not tolerable to owners," says Guy Tebbitt, vice president for research and development for Novartis Animal Health.

Also on January 5 the FDA gave the thumbs up to Pfizer's Anipryl, the first drug approved for doggie Alzheimer's. Pfizer sells a canine pain reliever and arthritis treatment as well, and late last year it announced an R&D program for medications that help pets with anxiety and dementia.

Another big player in the companion-animal field is Heska, a biotechnology firm based in Colorado that strives to increase the "quality of life" for cats and dogs. Its products include medicines for allergies and anxiety, as well as an antibiotic that fights periodontal disease. The company's Web site features a "spokesdog" named Perio Pooch and, like old "shock" movies from high school driver's-ed classes, a photograph of a diseased doggie mouth to demonstrate what can happen if teeth and gums are not treated carefully. No one wants pets to be in pain, and Heska also makes drugs for animal cancer, but it is a measure of priorities that US companies and their subsidiaries spend almost nothing on tropical diseases while, according to an industry source, they spend about half a billion dollars for R&D on animal health.

Although "companion animal" treatments are an extreme case—that half-billion-dollar figure covers "food animals" as well, and most veterinary drugs emerge from research on human medications—consider a few examples from the brave new world of human lifestyle drugs. Here, the pharmaceutical companies are scrambling to eradicate:

Impotence. Pfizer invested vast sums to find a cure for what Bob Dole and other industry spokesmen delicately refer to as "erectile dysfunction." The company hit the jackpot with Viagra, which racked up more than $1 billion in sales in its first year on the market. Two other companies, Schering-Plough and Abbott Laboratories, are already rushing out competing drugs.

Baldness. The top two drugs in the field, Merck's Propecia and Pharmacia & Upjohn's Rogaine (the latter sold over the counter), had combined sales of about $180 million in 1998. "Some lifestyle drugs are used for relatively serious problems, but even in the best cases we're talking about very different products from penicillin," says the retired drug company executive. "In cases like baldness therapy, we're not even talking about healthcare."

Toenail fungus. With the slogan "Let your feet get naked!" as its battle cry, pharmaceutical giant Novartis recently unveiled a lavish advertising campaign for Lamisil, a drug that promises relief for sufferers of this unsightly malady. It's a hot one, the war against fungus, pitting Lamisil against Janssen

Pharmaceutical's Sporanox and Pfizer's Diflucan for shares in a market estimated to be worth hundreds of millions of dollars a year.

Face wrinkles. Allergan earned $90 million in 1997 from sales of its "miracle" drug Botox. Injected between the eyebrows at a cost of about $1,000 for three annual treatments, Botox makes crow's feet and wrinkles disappear. "Every 7½ seconds someone is turning 50," a wrinkle expert told the *Dallas Morning News* in an article about Botox last year. "You're looking at this vast population that doesn't want frown lines."

Meanwhile, acute lower respiratory infections go untreated, claiming about 3.5 million victims per year, overwhelmingly children in poor nations. Such infections are third on the chart of the biggest killers in the world; the number of lives they take is almost half the total reaped by the number-one killer, heart disease, which usually strikes the elderly. "The development of new antibiotics," wrote drug company researcher A.J. Slater in a 1989 paper published in the Royal Society of Tropical Medicine and Hygiene's *Transactions,* "is very costly and their provision to Third World countries alone can never be financially rewarding."

In some cases, older medications thought to be unnecessary in the First World and commercially unviable in the Third have simply been pulled from the market. This created a crisis recently when TB re-emerged with a vengeance in US inner cities, since not a single company was still manufacturing Streptomycin after mid-1991. The FDA set up a task force to deal with the situation, but it was two years before it prodded Pfizer back into the field.

In 1990 Marion Merrell Dow (which was bought by German giant Hoechst in 1995) announced that it would manufacture Ornidyl, the first new medicine in forty years that was effective in treating African sleeping sickness. Despite the benign sounding name, the disease leads to coma and death, and kills about 40,000 people a year. Unlike earlier remedies for sleeping sickness, Ornidyl had few side effects. In field trials, it saved the lives of more than 600 patients, most of whom were near death. Yet Ornidyl was pulled from production; apparently company bean-counters determined that saving lives offered no return.

Because AIDS also plagues the First World, it is the one disease ravaging Third World countries that is the object of substantial drug company research. In many African countries, AIDS has wiped out a half-century of gains in child survival rates. In Botswana—a country that is not at war and has a relatively stable society—life expectancy rates fell by twenty years over a period of just five. In South Africa, the Health Ministry recently issued a report saying that 1,500 of the country's people are infected with HIV every day and predicting that the annual deathrate will climb to 500,000 within the next decade.

Yet available treatments and research initiatives offer little hope for poor people. A year's supply of the highly recommended multi-drug cocktail of three AIDS medicines costs about $15,000 a year. That's exorbitant in any part of the world, but prohibitive in countries like Uganda, where per capita income stands at $330. Moreover, different viral "families" of AIDS, with distinct immunological properties, appear in different parts of the world. About 85 percent of people with HIV live in the Third World, but industry research to develop an AIDS vaccine focuses only on the First World. "Without research dedicated to the specific viral strains that are prevalent in developing countries, vaccines for those countries will be very slow in coming," says Dr. Amir Attaran, an international expert who directs the Washington-based Malaria Project.

All the blame for the neglect of tropical diseases can't be laid at the feet of industry. Many Third World governments invest little in healthcare, and First World countries have slashed both foreign aid and domestic research programs. Meanwhile, the US government aggressively champions the interests of the drug industry abroad, a stance that often undermines healthcare needs in developing countries.

In one case where a drug company put Third World health before profit—Merck's manufacture of Ivermectin—governmental inertia nearly scuttled the good deed. It was the early eighties, and a Pakistani researcher at Merck discovered that the drug, until then used only in veterinary medicine, performed miracles in combating river blindness disease. With one dose per year of Ivermectin, people were fully protected from river blindness, which is carried by flies and, at the time, threatened hundreds of millions of people in West Africa.

Merck soon found that it would be impossible to market Ivermectin profitably, so in an unprecedented action the company decided to provide it free of charge to the WHO. (Vagelos, then chairman of Merck, said the company was worried about taking the step, "as we feared it would discourage companies from doing research relevant to the Third World, since they might be expected to follow suit.") Even then, the program nearly failed. The WHO claimed it didn't have the money needed to cover distribution costs, and Vagelos was unable to win financial support from the Reagan Administration. A decade after Ivermectin's discovery, only 3 million of 120 million people at risk of river blindness had received the drug. During the past few years, the WHO, the World Bank and private philanthropists have finally put up the money for the program, and it now appears that river blindness will become the second disease, after smallpox, to be eradicated.

Given the industry's profitability, it's clear that the companies could do far more. It's equally clear that they won't unless they are forced to. The success of ACT UP* in pushing drug companies to respond to the AIDS crisis in America is emblematic of how crucial but also how difficult it is to get the industry to budge. In late 1997, a coalition of public health organizations approached a group of major drug companies, including Glaxo-Wellcome and Roche, and asked them to fund a project that would dedicate itself to developing new treatments for major tropical diseases. Although the companies would have been required to put up no more than $2 million a year, they walked away from the table. Since there's no organized pressure—either from the grassroots or from governments—they haven't come back. "There [were] a number of problems at the business level," Harvey Bale, director of the Geneva-based International Federation of Pharmaceutical Manufacturers' Association, told *Science* magazine. "The cost of the project is high for some companies."

While the industry's political clout currently insures against any radical government action, even minor reforms could go a long way. The retired drug company executive points to public hospitals, which historically were guaranteed relatively high profit margins but were obligated to provide free care to the poor in return. There's also the example of phone companies, which charge businesses higher rates in order to subsidize universal service. "Society has tolerated high profit levels up until now, but society has the right to expect something back," he says. "Right now, it's not getting it."

The US government already lavishly subsidizes industry research and allows companies to market discoveries made by the National Institute of Health and other federal agencies. "All the government needs to do is start attaching some strings," says the Malaria Project's Attaran. "If a company wants to market another billion-dollar blockbuster, fine, but in exchange it will have to push through a new malaria drug. It will cost them some money, but it's not going to bankrupt them."

Eds. Note: AIDS Coalition to Unleash Power

Another type of "string" would be a "reasonable pricing" provision for drugs developed at federal laboratories. By way of explanation, Attaran recounted that the vaccine for hepatitis A was largely developed by researchers at the Walter Reed Army Institute. At the end of the day, the government gave the marketing rights to SmithKline Beecham and Merck. The current market for the vaccine, which sells for about $60 per person, is $300 million a year. The only thing Walter Reed's researchers got in exchange for their efforts was a plaque that hangs in their offices. "I'll say one thing for the companies," says Attaran. "They didn't skimp on the plaque; it's a nice one. But either the companies should have paid for part of the government's research, or they should have been required to sell the vaccine at a much lower price."

At the beginning of this year, Doctors Without Borders unveiled a campaign calling for increased access to drugs needed in Third World countries. The group is exploring ideas ranging from tax breaks for smaller firms engaged in research in the field, to creative use of international trade agreements, to increased donations of drugs from the multinational companies. Dr. Bernard Pécoul, an organizer of the campaign, says that different approaches are required for different diseases. In the case of those plaguing only the Southern Hemisphere—sleeping sickness, for example—market mechanisms won't work because there simply is no market to speak of. Hence, he suggests that if multinational firms are not willing to manufacture a given drug, they transfer the relevant technology to a Third World producer that is.

Drugs already exist for diseases that ravage the North as well as the South—AIDS and TB, for example—but they are often too expensive for people in the Third World. For twenty-five years, the WHO has used funding from member governments to purchase and distribute vaccines to poor countries; Pécoul proposes a similar model for drugs for tropical diseases. Another solution he points to: In the event of a major health emergency, state or private producers in the South would be allowed to produce generic versions of needed medications in exchange for a small royalty paid to the multinational license holder. "If we can't change the markets, we have to humanize them," Pécoul says. "Drugs save lives. They can't be treated as normal products."

◉ ◉ ◉

Questions

1. Why have drug companies focused almost exclusively on lifestyle drugs? What are some potential negative outcomes of this on the health of people throughout the world?

2. According to Silverstein, is it appropriate to put the blame solely on drug companies for their neglect of vaccines that would help people in Third World nations? Why, or why not?

3. The former head of Merck, Roy Vagelos said, "A corporation with stock-holders can't stoke up a laboratory that will focus on Third World diseases because it will go broke. That's a social problem, and industry shouldn't be expected to solve it." Do you agree or disagree with Mr. Vagelos? Why?

4. Visit the Doctors Without Borders website (www.doctorswithoutborders.org) and the World Health Organization website (www.who.int/homepage). What can one learn from these websites about world health problems and priorities? Is what you learned consistent with the claims made by Silverstein in this article? Explain.

Beyond Legalization: New Ideas for Ending the War on Drugs

MICHAEL MASSING

> According to Michael Massing, the United States' "war on
> drugs" has failed. The "solutions" that the U.S. government
> put in place did not stop the flow of illegal drugs into the
> United States, nor have they stopped people from selling and
> buying these substances.
>
> This selection features Massing's essay, from The Nation,
> which addresses the stubborn problem of illegal drug use in the
> United States. Then, three scholars respond to Massing. These
> authors review existing drug policies and offer new ideas for
> solutions that could be implemented in the war on drugs.

☺ It's Time for Realism

. . . The war on drugs has failed miserably. The clogging of our prisons with low-level drug offenders, the widespread curtailment of civil
liberties in the name of drug enforcement, the strained relations with
drug-producing nations to our south, the whole puritanical mindset
associated with Just Say No—all have contributed to a consensus on
the urgent need for change.

As to what that change should be, there are some clear areas of
agreement. Virtually all liberals, for instance, would like to see the

"Beyond Legalization: New Ideas for Ending the War on Drugs," by Michael Massing,
reprinted from The Nation, vol. 269, no. 8, 1999, pp. 11, 12, 14–16, 18–20.

police stop making so many drug arrests, which currently number more than 1.5 million a year. Everyone, too, would like to see an overhaul of the nation's harsh and discriminatory drug-sentencing laws—a step that would, among other things, reverse the relentless flow of black and Latino men into prison.

Beyond that, though, the consensus breaks down. And this has helped stall the movement for reform. Despite growing dissatisfaction with the drug war among the general public, progress toward change has been minimal, and the inability of liberals to propose a persuasive alternative helps explain why.

On the left, three schools of drug reform prevail. Each has something to offer but, by itself, is an inadequate guide to change. The most sensational is the CIA-trafficking school. . . . According to this perspective, America's drug problem cannot be fully understood without examining the CIA's periodic alliances with drug-running groups abroad, from the Hmong tribesmen in Laos to the *mujahedeen* in Afghanistan to the *contras* in Nicaragua. By teaming up with and providing cover to these forces, it is alleged, the CIA has facilitated the flow of drugs into the United States at critical moments. In the most eye-popping version of this theory, advanced by Gary Webb, traffickers linked to the CIA-backed *contras* are said to have supplied cocaine to major dealers in South Central Los Angeles, thus helping to set off the nation's crack epidemic. Though well aware of this activity, the CIA did nothing to intervene. (This theory was seized upon by some leaders of the black community, including Congresswoman Maxine Waters, who wrote a glowing foreword to Webb's book.)

With its chronicling of the CIA's ties to drug-tainted groups, the CIA-trafficking school deserves credit for exposing the hypocrisy of the drug war. It also raises important questions about the types of alliances the United States sometimes makes abroad. As a guide to drug reform, though, it's a dead end. However much the *contras* were involved in drug trafficking (and the evidence strongly suggests they were), they were clearly no more than bit players in the overall cocaine trade. If any one group was primarily responsible for the flow of cocaine into the United States, it was the Colombian traffickers, and no one has accused the CIA of abetting them. On the contrary, the US government has for the past fifteen years been waging all-out war on the Colombian narcos, with little to show for it.

Adherence to the CIA-trafficking school leads one into some strange policy terrain. In focusing so strongly on the intelligence agency, this school seems implicitly to accept the idea that Washington could actually do something about the flow of drugs into the United States if it really wanted to. If only the CIA would fight the traffickers, rather than shield them, it's implied, we could reduce the availability, and abuse, of drugs in this country. Yet, after thirty years of waging war on drugs, it should be apparent that with or without the CIA's help, the United States is incapable of stemming the flow of drugs into this country. The CIA-tracking school unwittingly bolsters the idea that the true source of America's drug problem lies outside our borders, and that the solution consists in cracking down on producers, processors and smugglers. In an odd way, then, this school actually reinforces the logic underlying the drug war.

By now, it should be clear that America's drug problem is homegrown, and that any effort to combat it must be centered here. In particular, we must confront the real source of our problem—the demand for drugs. On this point, many liberals subscribe to the "root causes" school. This holds that the problem of drug abuse in America reflects deeper ills in our society, such as poverty, unemployment, racial discrimination and urban neglect. To combat abuse, we must first address these underlying causes—through policies to promote full employment, increase the minimum wage, provide universal health insurance, end housing segregation and create opportunities for disadvantaged youths.

In focusing attention on the link between poverty and drug abuse, the root-causes school provides a valuable service. Studies indicate that drug addiction in the United States is disproportionately concentrated among the unemployed and under-educated. And certainly most liberals would endorse measures to improve their lot. This, however, takes us far beyond the realm of drug policy. To maintain that we must end poverty and discrimination in order to combat drug abuse seems a prescription for paralysis. The key is to find a strategy that is humane, affordable and sellable— to find a strategy, in short, that could actually work.

Certainly such a standard would seem to rule out the third main school of left/liberal drug reform—legalization. On the surface, drug legalization has undeniable appeal. If drugs were legalized, the vast criminal networks that distribute them, and that generate so much violence, would disappear. Prison space would be reserved for the truly dangerous, black motorists would no longer be stopped routinely on the New Jersey Turnpike, relations with countries like Mexico and Colombia would improve and Americans would no longer be hounded for the substances they decide to consume—a matter of personal choice.

Yet legalizing drugs would entail some serious risks, the most obvious being an increase in abuse. While legalizers tend to cite drug prohibition as the source of all evil when it comes to drugs, drugs themselves can cause extensive harm. Heroin, cocaine, crack and methamphetamine are highly toxic substances, and those addicted to them engage in all kinds of destructive behavior from preying on family members to assaulting strangers to abusing children. In all, there are an estimated 4 million hard-core drug users in the United States. Though making up only 20 percent of all drug users nationwide (the rest being occasional users) this group accounts for two-thirds to three-quarters of all the drugs consumed here. They also account for most of the crime, medical emergencies and other harmful consequences associated with drugs. If drugs were legalized, the number of chronic users could well increase.

History is full of cautionary examples. In the early seventies, for instance, doctors routinely began prescribing Valium (a minor tranquilizer) for everyday cases of anxiety. As the number of prescriptions increased, so did the incidence of abuse; by the late seventies Valium was sending more people to hospital emergency rooms than any other drug, heroin and cocaine included. As physicians became aware of Valium's dangers, they began writing fewer prescriptions for it, and the number of emergency cases began dropping as well. Clearly, making drugs easier to get can increase the extent to which they are abused, and one can only imagine what would happen if such potent intoxicants as heroin and crack suddenly became available by prescription or were sold openly. Under the regimes favored by some libertarians and free-marketeers, legalized drugs would be sold commercially and marketed aggressively, with potentially disastrous results for addicts and kids.

From a political standpoint, the liabilities of legalization are no less obvious. According to opinion polls, most Americans strongly oppose legalizing drugs. While the unpopularity of an idea should not automatically disqualify it, legalization seems a long-term loser. Indeed, the fact that legalization has so often been presented as the sole alternative to the drug war has hindered the movement for reform.

By now, the risks of legalization have become so evident that even onetime supporters no longer advocate it. Instead, they have embraced a variant of legalization called harm reduction. Not always easy to define, harm reduction generally holds that the primary goal of drug policy should not be to eliminate drug use but rather to reduce the harm that drugs cause. Those who can be persuaded to stop using drugs should be; those who can't should be encouraged to use their drugs more safely. To that end, harm reductionists favor expanding the availability of methadone, setting up needle-exchange programs, opening safe-injection rooms for heroin users and establishing heroin-maintenance programs that provide addicts with a daily dose of the drug.

There is much to admire in harm reduction. Its encouragement of tolerance for drug addicts provides a welcome alternative to the narrow moralism of the drug war. At times, though, harm reductionists take tolerance too far. In their eagerness to condemn the drug war, they sometimes fail to acknowledge the damage that drug addiction itself can inflict. While rightly condemning the political hysteria surrounding "crack babies," for instance, harm reductionists tend to overlook the havoc crack has wrought on inner-city families. And, while commendably calling for more needle-exchange programs, they rarely acknowledge that syringes are often handed out indiscriminately at these exchanges, with little effort to intervene with addicts and get them to address their habits.

Nonetheless, harm reduction—by recognizing that chronic users are at the core of the nation's drug problem and that they constitute a public-health rather than law-enforcement problem—can help point the way toward a more rational drug policy. The key is to develop a policy that is as tough on drug abuse as it is on the drug war.

In formulating such a policy, a good starting point is a 1994 RAND study that sought to compare the effectiveness of four different types of drug control: source-control programs (attacking the drug trade abroad), interdiction (stopping drugs at the border), domestic law enforcement (arresting and imprisoning buyers and sellers) and drug treatment. How much additional money, RAND asked, would the government have to spend on each approach to reduce national cocaine consumption by 1 percent? RAND devised a model of the national cocaine market, then fed into it more than seventy variables, from seizure data to survey responses. The results were striking: Treatment was found to be seven times more cost-effective than law enforcement, ten times more effective than interdiction and twenty-three times more effective than attacking drugs at their source.

The RAND study has generated much debate in drug-research circles, but its general conclusion has been confirmed in study after study. Yes, relapse is common, but, as RAND found, treatment is so inexpensive that it more than pays for itself while an individual is actually in a program, in the form of reduced crime, medical costs and the like; all gains that occur after an individual leaves a program are a bonus. And it doesn't matter what form of treatment one considers: methadone maintenance, long-term residential, intensive outpatient and twelve-step programs all produce impressive outcomes (though some programs work better for certain addicts than for others).

To be effective, though, treatment must be available immediately. Telling addicts who want help to come back the next day or week is a sure way to lose them. Unfortunately; in most communities, help is rarely available immediately; long waiting lists are the rule. In New York State alone, it is estimated that every year 100,000 people who would take advantage of drug or alcohol treatment if it were available are unable to get into a program.

Such numbers reflect the government's spending priorities. Of the $18 billion Washington spends annually to fight drugs, fully two-thirds goes to reduce the supply of drugs and just one-third to reduce the demand. In all, less than 10 percent of federal funds go to treat the hard-core users, who constitute the real heart of the problem. Closing the nation's treatment gap should be a top priority for the government.

How can we make this happen? According to federal estimates, the government would have to spend about $3.4 billion a year on top of current treatment expenditures to make help available to all who want it; the states would have to spend roughly an equivalent amount. If the current 67/33 percent split in the federal drug budget between the supply and demand sides were equalized, this would free up close to the sum in question at the federal level. Actually, a strong case could be made for reversing these proportions and allocating two-thirds to the demand side, but a 50/50 split seems as much as can be hoped for in the current political climate.

Finding a more effective means of preventing drug use among young people is another urgent need. Today, prevention consists mainly of Just Say No messages broadcast on TV or preached in the classroom. Unfortunately, research shows that such messages by themselves do not work. To succeed, prevention, like treatment, needs to focus on those most at risk. The problem is not so much with kids who smoke an occasional joint but with those who regularly use drugs and/or alcohol. For youths living in poor neighborhoods, effective prevention would mean more recreational programs, after-school activities and summer job opportunities (a key plank of the root-causes school). For more privileged students, prevention might take the form of early-warning systems in which teachers, counselors and parents work together to intervene with youths who show signs of getting into trouble with drugs, legal or otherwise.

As for the nation's drug laws, the goal should not be abolishing them—keeping drugs illegal can help contain abuse—but making them more rational so that small-time offenders are not hit with excessive penalties. And, whenever possible, nonviolent addicts and sellers who are arrested should be offered treatment as an alternative to incarceration. More generally, arresting low-level offenders should be society's last, not first, line of defense.

A word on marijuana. At present, almost 700,000 people a year are arrested for the sale or possession of pot. This is madness. Marijuana is far less toxic than heroin, cocaine or even alcohol, and the idea of putting people in jail for possessing it seems absurd. At the same time, marijuana is not innocuous, especially for young people, and we do not want to do anything that would make it even more available than it is now. Legalizing marijuana would certainly risk that. A far more rational approach would be to decriminalize the drug; people caught using pot in public would be subject to a civil penalty punishable by a fine, much as a traffic violation is. The production, importation and sale of marijuana, however, would remain illegal (though not subject to the ridiculously harsh penalties now in place). Decriminalization offers a realistic middle ground between the excesses of our current approach and the potential perils of legalization.

In my recent book *The Fix*, I argue that a public-health approach to the drug problem can work based on the one time we actually tried it—during the Nixon Administration. Nixon, a staunch law-and-order advocate, is remembered for having launched the war on drugs, but, drawing on his pragmatic instincts, he in fact made treatment his main weapon in that war. Confronting a national heroin epidemic, the White House created a special action office headed by physicians and addiction specialists, who spent hundreds of millions of dollars to set up a national network of clinics that offered help to all those who wanted it. The result was a marked decline in heroin-related crime, overdose deaths and hospital emergency-room visits. The national heroin epidemic was thus stanched.

Unfortunately, that network largely disintegrated during the Reagan years, so that by the time crack struck, treatment clinics were completely overwhelmed. Today, our drug problem is far larger and more complex than it was under Nixon. But the research confirming treatment's effectiveness has grown, too, and in light of the ongoing failure of the drug war, a public-health approach stressing treatment over prosecution, counseling over incarceration, would seem to offer our most humane, practical and politically viable alternative.

❧ Life of a Scandal

Peter Kornbluh Replies

In mid-October 1996, two months after the publication of Gary Webb's series "Dark Alliance" in the San Jose Mercury News, an extraordinary town meeting took place in Compton, California, one of the South Central neighborhoods of LA ravaged by the crack epidemic. A daylong series of panels, convened by Representative Juanita Millender-McDonald, examined many of the critical issues related to drug use and abuse—the human casualties of crack-related crime, gang operations, sentencing inequities, police corruption and, of course, the brewing CIA-contra-cocaine scandal.

One witness could not be physically present. The voice of "Freeway" Ricky Ross, serving life without parole for his activities as LA's most renowned crack dealer in the eighties, was piped in over the loudspeakers. Ross, who received some of his coke from a Nicaraguan trafficker whom Webb identified as a CIA-backed contra, clearly had the sympathy of the 800 people who filled the audience. When he told Representative Millender-McDonald that Ronald Reagan and George Bush "deserve to be in jail with me," the crowd cheered its approval.

The surreal nature of Ross's participation in this forum—the man whom the Los Angeles Times once called "the one outlaw capitalist most responsible for flooding Los Angeles streets with mass-marketed cocaine" being hailed as a victim rather than the foremost victimizer illustrates at least a temporary distortion in the debate over drug policy that Michael Massing attributes to the CIA-trafficking scandal. In this case, the focus and outrage of the audience was directed away from the criminal damage wrought by a member of the community and toward the amorphous specter of CIA and US government misconduct. Across the country, immediately following the publication of the "Dark Alliance" series, thousands of activists, community leaders and citizens vented their rage at the CIA's "responsibility" for drugs flowing into the inner cities.

But the agenda of those who helped to expose this scandal was to highlight the government's criminal abuse of power and gross distortion of social and political priorities during the cold war—not to find a solution to the scourge of drugs in our society. By suggesting that they constitute a "main school" of thought on drug reform, or even a "tendency" on the left, Massing is creating a straw-man argument—itself a diversion in the drug debate.

With one exception, the main writings and reports on the reprehensible merging of covert operations and drug trafficking during the CIA's Third World wars have never offered prescriptions for drug policy. The Senate Subcommittee on Terrorism, Narcotics and International Operations, led by Senator John Kerry, documented government knowledge of and tolerance for drug smuggling under the guise of national security; Gary Webb's book (drawn from his series) is a journalistic account of the CIA-backed *contras*, cocaine smuggling and corruption and competition among law-enforcement agencies in California; the Alexander Cockburn/Jeffrey St. Clair book, *Whiteout: The CIA, Drugs and the Press*, was about just what its title suggests.

Only Alfred McCoy, in his seminal work, *The Politics of Heroin: CIA Complicity in the Global Drug Trade,* concluded with policy analysis and recommendations to confront the crisis. Contrary to Massing's argument that, for the CIA-crack "tendency," "the solution consists in cracking down on producers, processors and smugglers," McCoy writes: "Simply put, narcotics are major global commodities resistant to any attempt at localized suppression. As long as the demand for drugs in the cities of the First World continues to grow, Third World producers will find a way to supply their markets." He agrees with Massing that legalization would expand drug use and abuse, particularly among teenagers. His "middle ground" solution, worth considering in the context of this discussion, is "regulation"—a combination of emphasizing (1) treatment and education to reduce demand, (2) short-term interdiction to reduce but not eliminate shipments bound for the United States, (3) multilateral efforts through the UN aimed at reducing global supply and (4) barring CIA protection of drug smugglers in the name of covert operations.

Likewise, the vast majority of political and social activists working on drug reform have not allowed the scandal to dominate their agenda or distort their priorities; rather, they have used it to increase public interest in reconsidering other aspects of the "war on drugs." Even at the Compton meeting, the CIA debate helped draw attention to issues like drug-related violence that might not otherwise have received such scrutiny. In the aftermath of the scandal, the Institute for Policy Studies created a Citizens' Fact-finding Commission on US Drug Policy. Its first meeting, held in Los Angeles in May, covered everything from the CIA-crack scandal to the social costs of the drug war and how the drug economy functions, and examined policy alternatives such as harm reduction. And when the Congressional Black Caucus, chaired by Representative Maxine Waters, drew up its agenda last year, the goal of "investigating allegations of involvement in drug trafficking by intelligence agencies" was the last of six CBC objectives, including:

- Increase funding for drug prevention, treatment and education for at-risk communities.

- Refocus federal resources to target and punish large-scale drug smugglers, suppliers and distributors.

- Propose enhanced sentences for law-enforcement personnel convicted of drug-related offenses.

- Organize town-hall meetings, workshops and educational forums to take our drug-eradication message to communities across the nation.
- Eliminate sentencing disparities.

The CIA-*contra*-crack scandal remains a salient issue of history and accountability—one that will not be fully laid to rest until Congress bars the CIA from secretly putting traffickers on the US payroll. As a confidence-building measure with the public, the agency must also declassify all documentation on its sordid relations with drug traffickers posing as freedom fighters. Full disclosure, along with a concrete apology, would not be just an academic exercise. The lasting impact of this scandal is not that it distracted the left from engaging in the drug policy reform debate but that, throughout the communities most affected by the horrors of drug abuse, it has reinforced cynicism and skepticism about the willingness of the US government to address this issue credibly and fulfill its responsibility to protect our citizens from true threats to their security and well-being.

◎ Perils of Prohibition

Mike Gray Replies

Over the years Michael Massing has done a highly effective job of reporting on America's various drug war failures, but he now seems unable to face his own facts. While admitting that the drug war is a disaster on almost every front, he seems to be trying to tell us that we can still pull it out by giving it a kinder face—that if, somehow, we can make the penalties less draconian and get everybody into treatment, we can save the present system.

Unfortunately, the system Massing supports was doomed at its inception, and the fix he proposes is a Band-Aid. He leaves the cancer of prohibition intact, a policy that created the drug problem in the first place and has made it steadily worse. Today, even a casual glance at the prison stats reveals that, by accident or design, the drug war has turned into a race war.

Massing himself itemizes the advantages of ending drug prohibition—the violent global criminal networks would dry up, we could go back to building colleges instead of prisons, the Bill of Rights would actually mean something again—but these remarkable benefits are countered in his mind by the specter of addiction sweeping the land. He warns that if we call off the police dogs there could be an explosion of addicts. And while that might sound logical, our own history and the European experience suggests otherwise.

When alcohol prohibition in the United States crashed and burned in 1933, drug prohibition should have ended with it for the same reasons—the corruption, the gunplay, the judicial paralysis—but there simply were not and never have been enough drug users to form a political constituency. This is an essential fact the prohibitionists can't seem to grasp: Hard drugs don't have that much appeal and never did. Before 1914, both drugs and alcohol were legal, and almost nobody did drugs (three-tenths of 1 percent of the population). After 1919, both drugs and alcohol were illegal, and almost nobody did drugs.

In fact, drugs and alcohol had come to be considered déclassé by the wealthy, and their use across the board was in rapid decline—a testament to the success of the temperance movement. Then the moral leaders decided to make their victory absolute and call in the cops. What had been unfashionable suddenly became exotic: If you didn't have a hip flask in 1920 you were a nobody. And even though there were probably fewer than 300,000 narcotics addicts in the whole country, we decided to root them out. Today, after an eighty-year, trillion-dollar *jihad*, the total number of addicts is up around 4 million. Instead of decreasing the rate of addiction, we gave it a five-fold boost.

While our repressive policies have been creating addicts, other countries have been abandoning our approach in favor of tolerance, and the results have been dramatic. Twenty years ago—about the time the United States started getting really serious about marijuana prohibition—the Dutch decided to go the other way. They made marijuana freely available to anyone over 16 (later it was raised to 18).

Horrified American experts predicted that pot use in the Netherlands would skyrocket, but they were confounded. It is the American students who are now smoking significantly more pot than the Dutch. What's more, our teenagers say marijuana is easier to get than beer. Why? Because beer distribution is controlled by the state—you have to be 18 and prove it. Marijuana distribution is controlled by some guy in a house across town who sells to your neighbor's kid, no ID required.

There's a similar contrast in the way our two countries have handled the heroin problem. Twenty years ago, the average age of a heroin user in the United States was 25. It was about the same in Holland. But while we dedicated ourselves to harassing heroin addicts in a national game of fox and hounds, the Dutch offered support, assistance, a place to shoot up and a chance to be left alone as long as you didn't create a public nuisance. Today, the average age of a heroin user in Holland is 36—ten years older. Which means young people in the Netherlands are losing interest in the drug. But in the United States, where our zero-tolerance policies were supposed to have stamped out this scourge by 1995, the average age of a heroin user has dropped to 19. The most recent jump here is among eighth graders.

On the positive side, Massing rightly praises treatment, the one option that actually produces results, but he would limit his tolerance to methadone, a synthetic substitute for heroin. This treatment is guaranteed to miss that huge cohort of serious heroin users who commit most of the crime and on whom the black market depends. These people would rather go to prison than be forced into treatment. In prison they can get heroin.

The Swiss government recently conducted an experiment with 1,000 of these hard-core heroin addicts to see what would happen if doctors simply gave them the stuff along with some support services. Crime dropped by 60 percent, homelessness was eliminated, half the unemployed found jobs and a third of the welfare cases became self-supporting. But most important, by the end of the experiment eighty-three addicts had decided on their own to give up heroin in favor of abstinence. This is a better cure rate than most of our zero-tolerance programs have. It turns out that whether we give users the drugs with a box of needles or chain them up and force them into detox, somewhere between 5 and 10 percent a year will give them up.

As for marijuana, Massing acknowledges that it's less harmful than alcohol; then he offers us another Band-Aid. Decriminalization—arresting the sellers but not the buyers—is exactly what we were doing during alcohol prohibition. You could drink all you wanted, you just couldn't make it or buy it. That setup gave us Al Capone, the St. Valentine's Day massacre and institutional corruption on a scale never imagined before then.

In the end, Massing's argument rests on the widely held but flawed assumption that prohibition is holding down the number of drug users. "What would happen," he asks, if heroin and crack suddenly were "sold openly"? One wonders where he's been living. Right now anyone—any 14-year-old—who wants drugs can usually find them within minutes almost anywhere in the country. Because of the staggering profits driving distribution, illegal drugs have market penetration that rivals Coca-Cola. If you don't believe it, ask the next cop you run into.

Legalization, a concept Massing seems to equate with crack vending machines in the lunchroom, is in fact the only way out of this nightmare. Legalization means regulation, not chaos. Chaos is what we've got now. Legalization means state control instead of mob control. It's the only hope we have for getting the drug trade off the street and out of the hands of our children.

☺ Yes, Treatment, But . . .
Elliott Currie Replies

Michael Massing has written thoughtfully about the follies of American drug policy in the past, and I'm sympathetic to many things he says in this piece. It's true that progressives have often been unhappily divided over what to do about drugs, and that there has been an inadequate appreciation of the costs of drug abuse itself—as opposed to the costs of the drug war—among some of the left. And certainly, like most people I know, I think we need to shift toward more treatment and prevention, less incarceration and interdiction. But I find Massing's argument here less than convincing as a manifesto for a progressive drug policy, for a number of reasons.

One is the tendency to treat the several "main schools" of drug reform as if they were mutually exclusive, and in the process to caricature them. Since I'm probably one of those Massing has in mind when he talks about the "root causes" school . . ., I'll focus on that, though I think the problem also applies to his discussion of legalization and harm reduction.

There's more than a little straw-manning here; adherents of the "root-causes school" are said to believe that we must "first" deal with poverty and other social ills before we can do anything else about drugs, and then are accordingly dismissed as politically quixotic. But nobody I know actually says that. Certainly I don't. When I wrote a book about drugs a few years ago, I said we need a multilayered approach; we need better treatment, more harm-reduction programs, selective decriminalization, more creative adolescent prevention efforts and much more—all in the context of a broader "strategy of inclusion" that would systematically tackle the misery and hopelessness that, as study after study shows, has bred the worst drug abuse in America and elsewhere. That strategy involves investing in, among other things, family support centers, apprenticeship programs, paid family leaves, high-quality childcare and a lot else.

I didn't say we should provide these things instead of drug treatment, and I don't know anyone who has. For the life of me, I can't fathom how this amounts to a "prescription for paralysis." I'm frankly mystified by the argument that says we should talk about drug treatment rather than job training or a decent housing policy or family support. . . . Why not acknowledge that we need to move on all of these fronts in a comprehensive attack on drug abuse?

Massing's answer is, in part, that doing so would take us beyond the purview of "drug policy." Yep, it would; that's precisely why we need to do it. To say we can successfully attack the drug problem through "drug policy" alone is like saying we can solve the illness problem through the healthcare system alone—which we increasingly understand is the wrong way to think about health and illness. Or like saying that we can eliminate crime through the criminal justice system alone, which has helped to give us the biggest prison system in the world. It isn't, after all, differences in the availability of treatment that account for the wide differences in chronic hard-drug abuse between countries—why, for example, crack utterly devastated inner cities in the United States but had a far more muted impact in other industrial countries like Canada, Australia and the Netherlands.

So rather than counterposing separate "schools" of reform, we ought to be crafting an approach to drugs that operates on several levels at once. In that approach, of course, treatment should have a very important place. But we need to think about treatment more critically than Massing does.

It's true that drug treatment was unfairly maligned for a long time; it's also true that the public treatment system is sorely underfunded in many places. But that doesn't mean that throwing money at the existing treatment system amounts to a progressive drug policy. As it stands, the treatment available ranges from the highly effective to the utterly bogus. It needs to be reformed as well as expanded, and reformed in ways that make it more user-friendly for those who need help and more capable of addressing the complex social needs that addicts bring to treatment.

Drug treatment does indeed work under some conditions, but it works much better for some people than for others. Great numbers of addicts, moreover, including many of those with the most serious problems, never go into treatment at all—not because no treatment exists but because they don't want it. Of those who do go, great numbers drop out, especially in the "therapeutic community" programs, which often boast, on the surface, the best records of success (this tends to inflate our assessments of the effectiveness of treatment, which are typically based on the fraction of addicts who not only enter it but actually complete it). Nor is this lack of enthusiasm mysterious: Much of what passes for treatment today is woefully inadequate at best and deeply alienating at worst. It's often worst of all for women and the young. I used to work in a drug treatment program. Some of the "treatment" I saw I wouldn't wish on anybody—nor would I spend a dime of the public's money to buy more of it.

Treatment works best when it's linked to broader efforts to improve addicts' lives. And that suggests, again, why it's so unhelpful to separate treatment from social intervention—from "root causes." Over and over again, the research on treatment tells us that what makes long-run success likely is the realistic opportunity for a better and more stable life: a steady job, a family, a home, a future. Without that, treatment is all too often a revolving door. So treatment programs need to be linked to job training and placement, to family support, to housing advocacy. The best programs do this now, and in these comprehensive programs it's very difficult to define where "treatment" leaves off and intervention into "root causes" begins.

What progressives ought to be supporting, in short, is not "treatment" but those models of treatment that really work to change addicts' prospects over the long haul, and that embody humane values that we can wholeheartedly support. My guess is that Massing wouldn't disagree with that, but if I'm right, I wish he'd say so. And I think these caveats are especially crucial now, because we've seen a significant turn toward treatment in the past few years. The quick spread of treatment-oriented drug courts is probably the biggest piece of that shift, but there is also the remarkable Arizona initiative, which substitutes treatment for prison sentences for low-level offenders. Even "drug czar" Gen. Barry McCaffrey now says we should invest more in treatment. But the new acceptance of treatment has rarely been backed by much concern for whether the programs we're offering are any good, and if so, for whom.

So let us, by all means, work to close the "treatment gap." But let's also insist on closing the equally consequential gap between the crummy reality of too much of the treatment we now have and the treatment we could have if we took treatment and its clients more seriously. And let's insist on better living standards for the urban and rural dispossessed, so that we can truly reduce the demand for hard drugs—and the need for treatment—over the long haul.

Michael Massing Responds

I'm encouraged to see how much common ground there is between my colleagues and me. But some key differences remain.

Peter Kornbluh contends that the distorting effect of all those CIA exposes is temporary, that in the long run they reinforce popular cynicism about government policy, but this seems naive. John Kerry's investigation into US drug policy in Central America may have helped dramatize the hypocrisy of the drug war, but it also built support for the invasion of Panama. Gary Webb's work may have convinced the Institute for Policy Studies to create a citizens' fact-finding commission on US drug policy, but it also gave rise to meetings like the one in Compton that Kornbluh describes. That the audience felt driven to cheer a major crack dealer like Ricky Ross vividly illustrates my point about the warping effect these exposés have had.

As Kornbluh candidly notes, most of the authors of these exposes don't really care about the drug issue. They're interested in it only to the extent that it can contribute to their efforts to expose US covert activities abroad. This seems cynical in its own right. That said, I welcome Kornbluh's assurance that the investigators of CIA drug-running endorse an enlightened package of drug policy reform.

Mike Gray makes several assertions that taken as gospel by legalizers—are nonetheless highly dubious. One is his farfetched contention that prohibition created the drug problem in the first place. The entrenched poverty in our inner cities seems a far more important cause. I also question his assertion that it's easier for teenagers to get marijuana than beer. Anyone who visits a bar near a college campus can attest to how readily available alcohol is to minors. The notoriously lax state regulation of alcohol sales to minors seems a poor model for drug distribution. As for adults, most cannot find heroin or crack within hours, much less minutes; to assert that such drugs have a market penetration rivaling Coca-Cola is preposterous. Even those who do know where to find hard drugs are often deterred by the fear of arrest. And without such a deterrent, it seems reason-

157

able to assume that more Americans would use, and abuse, these drugs.

As for the Dutch, they have not legalized heroin; they have fought it with the types of treatment and prevention programs I advocate in my essay. I agree with Gray that the Swiss heroin-maintenance experiment is promising and should probably be tested here. To qualify for the Swiss program, though, one must be a chronic addict. That leaves the question of how to deal with people addicted to other drugs, like cocaine, as well as with those not addicted at all. How should drugs be made available to these users? Gray—like so many advocates of legalization—offers few specifics.

I agree with most of what Elliott Currie has to say. In my book *The Fix*, I discuss at length the need to provide not only more treatment but better treatment. I wholeheartedly agree that treatment programs work best when joined to broader efforts to improve addicts' lives through the provision of steady jobs, affordable housing and the like. Currie loses me, however, when he engages in rhetorical flights about the need to fight misery and hopelessness and to raise living standards for the dispossessed—not because I oppose such goals, but because casting the issue so grandly makes real reform all the more difficult. Imagine being asked to testify before a state or Congressional panel about drug reform. How far is one likely to get talking about the need for paid family leave, quality childcare and national health insurance? I think it would be far more effective to discuss the need to ease drug penalties, reduce the number of drug arrests, make treatment more available and improve the quality of treatment.

With each passing month, more and more Americans become disillusioned with the drug war and open to a new approach. To gain favor, though, that approach must (1) be tough on drug abuse, (2) be narrowly focused on the drug issue and (3) have a real chance of working. I believe that the public-health strategy I have described— away from punishment and toward rehabilitation (in the broad sense Elliott Currie advocates)—offers our best chance of success.

☺ ☺ ☺

Questions

1. Massing presents three schools of thought on drug policy reform held by the Left. Describe each of these schools of thought. Which one does he argue is most promising?

2. What is "harm reduction"? How likely is this policy to succeed?

3. Briefly summarize the arguments made by Kornbluh, Gray, and Currie. Which of these arguments is most similar to your own?

4. Write your own response to Massing's arguments about how to end the war on drugs.